50 STRATEGIES for Teaching STEAM Skills

Kara Ball

Publishing Credits

Corinne Burton, M.A.Ed., *President and Publisher*
Aubrie Nielsen, M.S.Ed., *EVP of Content Development*
Kyra Ostendorf, M.Ed., *Publisher, Professional Books*
James Anderson, M.S.Ed., *VP of Digital Product*
Véronique Bos, *VP of Creative*
Tom Rademacher, M.Ed., *Developmental Editor*
Cassie Sitzman, *Editor*
Kevin Pham, *Graphic Designer*

Image Credits

Photographs on pages 17, 21, 35, 47, 51, 59, 69, 75, 78 , 81, and 82 by Maria Zuchora-Walske. All others Shutterstock.

A division of Teacher Created Materials
5482 Argosy Avenue
Huntington Beach, CA 92649
www.tcmpub.com/shell-education
ISBN 979-8-8855-4339-2
© 2024 Shell Educational Publishing, Inc.

Table of Contents

Welcome

STEAM (science, technology, engineering, arts, and mathematics) education is not new, but its importance continues to grow. STEAM education provides students with the skills necessary to succeed today and excel tomorrow. Although STEAM has been gaining popularity for years, guidance for educators on how to get started with it is still sparse. This book provides fifty standalone strategies that teachers can do with students in grades PK–12. The strategies are bundled into five sections that each focus on an essential STEAM skill: creativity, communication, collaboration, critical thinking, and, most important, failing. Each section includes ten strategies that give students an opportunity to build the skill.

This book is born from the work of countless educators who recognized the importance of providing their students with STEAM experiences and began creating activities to do so. Over the years, I have worked with other STEAM educators to identify and create activities that could be done in a single class period or extended over multiple days. I led professional learning sessions with hundreds of educators, building a community with them and collaborating around ideas that would become the foundation for the strategies in this book.

This collection of strategies is not exhaustive. Every day, teachers are sharing creative and innovative ideas for how to engage students in STEAM. It is, however, a collection of activities I have used in my work as a STEAM teacher, curriculum writer, and coordinator to build essential skills for STEAM learning.

The resources and information about STEAM education are ever-growing and evolving. Be a part of this conversation. Make these strategies your own and inspire your students to be the inventors and innovators of today, tomorrow, and the future.

—Kara Ball

Tips and Practices for Getting Started with STEAM

Implementing any new strategy can be hard, but there are things you can do to make getting started with STEAM a little easier. As you make your way through the strategies in this book, focus on encouraging students to take reasonable risks, to try new ideas, and to explore the unknown. Emphasize the importance of staying within the criteria or constraints over being "right" or "perfect." Give students opportunities to work alone, with partners, and on teams or in groups. You might even want to set up an area in the classroom to collect recyclables for use in the activities and designate a space for common supplies like scissors, tape, glue, crayons, and paper.

Young people are naturally curious, and STEAM is a wonderful way to engage them in learning about the world they live in and considering the possibilities for the world they will someday create. We can tap into that curiosity by connecting STEAM activities to students' lives and engaging in real-world problem-solving.

As you work through the strategies, you'll notice some overarching key practices. These practices help engage and motivate students to be active participants in STEAM learning. They include:

- providing real-world problems and authentic learning experiences
- giving students voice and choice
- using performance-based assessment
- offering opportunities for hands-on experiential learning
- using inquiry-based instruction
- fostering curiosity
- encouraging cooperative learning

You can incorporate these strategies into any part of your day. When I was in the classroom, I found the end of the day to be a wonderful time for STEAM activities. This allowed me to use STEAM as an incentive for the day and as motivation for students to work on subjects they might otherwise avoid. If there was an activity that needed to sit overnight, it was easy to leave at the end of the day without disrupting other instructional blocks. If you aren't able to set aside a dedicated time block for STEAM in your schedule, you might create a STEAM station or center in your classroom instead.

Also consider these questions when planning STEAM activities:

- Where will I store supplies and materials?
- What materials can students have access to without direct supervision?
- How will students collect and gather materials for activities?
- What grouping strategies will I use for group activities?
- Where can the students work?
- How will students document their work?
- Is there an area in the school building to display student creations?
- During activities that require additional adult support, how will I find volunteers?

How to Use This Resource

The strategies in this book are organized into five sections that each focus on a specific STEAM skill: failing, creativity, communication, collaboration, and critical thinking. Each section includes ten strategies to help students build the skill. You can choose to work through a section by having your students complete each strategy. Or you can choose a strategy at random and give it a whirl. However you make your way through the individual strategies, be sure to review materials lists ahead of time. Most activities use common items found in schools and classrooms, but there are some where you'll likely need to gather additional materials.

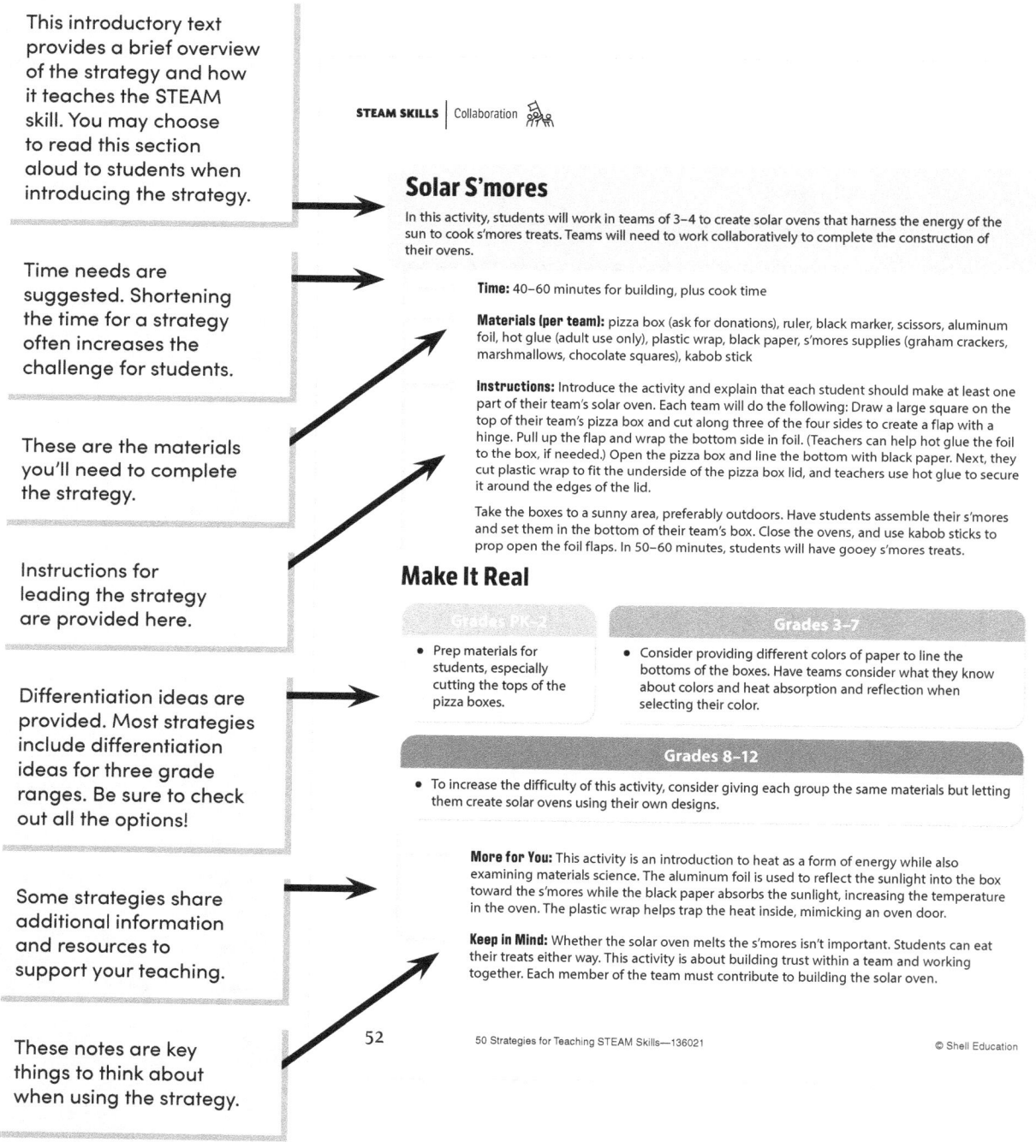

This introductory text provides a brief overview of the strategy and how it teaches the STEAM skill. You may choose to read this section aloud to students when introducing the strategy.

Time needs are suggested. Shortening the time for a strategy often increases the challenge for students.

These are the materials you'll need to complete the strategy.

Instructions for leading the strategy are provided here.

Differentiation ideas are provided. Most strategies include differentiation ideas for three grade ranges. Be sure to check out all the options!

Some strategies share additional information and resources to support your teaching.

These notes are key things to think about when using the strategy.

STEAM SKILLS | Collaboration

Solar S'mores

In this activity, students will work in teams of 3–4 to create solar ovens that harness the energy of the sun to cook s'mores treats. Teams will need to work collaboratively to complete the construction of their ovens.

Time: 40–60 minutes for building, plus cook time

Materials (per team): pizza box (ask for donations), ruler, black marker, scissors, aluminum foil, hot glue (adult use only), plastic wrap, black paper, s'mores supplies (graham crackers, marshmallows, chocolate squares), kabob stick

Instructions: Introduce the activity and explain that each student should make at least one part of their team's solar oven. Each team will do the following: Draw a large square on the top of their team's pizza box and cut along three of the four sides to create a flap with a hinge. Pull up the flap and wrap the bottom side in foil. (Teachers can help hot glue the foil to the box, if needed.) Open the pizza box and line the bottom with black paper. Next, they cut plastic wrap to fit the underside of the pizza box lid, and teachers use hot glue to secure it around the edges of the lid.

Take the boxes to a sunny area, preferably outdoors. Have students assemble their s'mores and set them in the bottom of their team's box. Close the ovens, and use kabob sticks to prop open the foil flaps. In 50–60 minutes, students will have gooey s'mores treats.

Make It Real

Grades PK–2	Grades 3–7
• Prep materials for students, especially cutting the tops of the pizza boxes.	• Consider providing different colors of paper to line the bottoms of the boxes. Have teams consider what they know about colors and heat absorption and reflection when selecting their color.

Grades 8–12
• To increase the difficulty of this activity, consider giving each group the same materials but letting them create solar ovens using their own designs.

More for You: This activity is an introduction to heat as a form of energy while also examining materials science. The aluminum foil is used to reflect the sunlight into the box toward the s'mores while the black paper absorbs the sunlight, increasing the temperature in the oven. The plastic wrap helps trap the heat inside, mimicking an oven door.

Keep in Mind: Whether the solar oven melts the s'mores isn't important. Students can eat their treats either way. This activity is about building trust within a team and working together. Each member of the team must contribute to building the solar oven.

52   50 Strategies for Teaching STEAM Skills—136021   © Shell Education

Skill 1: Failing Your Way to Success

Failure is often considered to be a bad thing—the opposite of success and certainly best avoided. However, most people experience failure far more often than they do success, and we usually learn a lot from our failures.

When I teach students about failure, I like to describe it as "not meeting an objective" or "not having the desired outcome." But this doesn't necessarily mean that what occurs is bad. Sometimes, and maybe even most times, failure is an important teacher—showing us where we went wrong and what we might do differently when we try again.

The Role of the Teacher

Students are going to experience a lot of failure when trying to complete the STEAM activities in this and subsequent skills. That's good! Let failure happen, and help students accept and learn from it. We don't want students to fear failure. Rather, we want them to view it as an opportunity to learn from mistakes and improve. This ability to view failure as a step toward success is directly connected to an ability to persist when challenged.

So when failures happen, remind students that it's okay to make mistakes. If a student is getting frustrated, support them by asking what worked, what didn't work, and what they could try differently. You can also encourage them to seek help from peers and get a second opinion. Resiliency in failure is an important skill in the classroom and beyond.

Failing as a STEAM Skill

No one—not scientists, artists, programmers, or teachers—gets everything right on the first try. Learning to cope with (and even celebrate) failing is an important skill and can help students understand why and how to make the most of it when things go wrong.

The strategies in this chapter are designed so that students experience failure. As you complete them, keep an eye out for opportunities to celebrate, learn from, and persevere through mistakes. Here are some helpful things you can do in these moments.

Share examples of famous failures and mistakes. For example, in 1968, a chemist named Spencer Silver was trying to create a superstrong adhesive for the aerospace industry, but his experiments resulted in a very weak glue. Six years later, another scientist who worked with Silver got annoyed at bookmarks that kept falling out of books and used some of Silver's glue on small sheets of paper. Since then, the Post-it Note has become one of the most popular office supplies in the world. Sharing this and other famous failures can help students begin to see failure as a stepping stone toward success. Can students think of any times in their lives when something good came from a mess-up?

Model how to cope with failure. You might tell a story of a time you felt disappointed when something didn't go to plan or use an example from a popular movie or book. Be sure to share how you or the character kept trying in these situations. It's also good to talk about the real cost of the failure ("It wasn't as bad as it felt because . . .") and model how you reframe it into a first step ("It helped me think about . . .").

Share the FAIL acronym. How can students reframe when they FAIL? By recognizing failures as a **F**irst **A**ttempt **I**n **L**earning. Teach students this acronym and refer to it whenever they struggle, helping them internalize its message. ("It didn't work? Great! What did you learn from it? What can we try next?") Being upbeat and celebrating failure as a first step in learning can help students see mistakes in a more positive light.

Leaning Tower of Pasta

Working together in teams of 3–4, students will build the tallest possible spaghetti-noodle tower that can hold the weight of one marshmallow. Spaghetti noodles are not a strong material and are subject to breaking. This can be frustrating for students, but it's important for them to persist in building their towers despite the challenges that come from working with this unconventional material.

Time: 10–25 minutes for building, plus measuring time

Materials (per team): dry spaghetti noodles, masking tape, string, ruler, scissors, marshmallow

Instructions: Introduce the activity. Avoid showing examples of towers since students may mimic the designs. Give teams time to build their towers. When time is up, allow teams to view each other's designs. Measure each team's tower to determine which is the tallest. Talk about the failures teams experienced in building their towers and what they did when failures happened.

Make It Real

Grades PK–2

- Give younger students only 10–12 noodles at a time to encourage them to be careful with the materials and reduce waste. They can ask for more noodles if needed.

Grades 3–7

- Provide students with the option to measure the height of their towers themselves.

Grades 8–12

- After measuring all teams' towers, determine the average, mean, and median heights.
- If a tie for the tallest tower occurs, conduct a tiebreaker using extra marshmallows. The winning tower is the one that holds the most marshmallow weight.

More for You: Consider conducting this activity as a schoolwide challenge and sharing the results on a school bulletin board.

Keep in Mind: Many students, especially as they get older, worry about making mistakes or failing when presented with a challenge. They may be reluctant to try creative ideas and hesitant to speak up within their teams. Dedicate some time at the end of this activity to discussing what successful teams did, emphasizing that worrying about failure decreases the odds of experiencing success.

Geronimo!

In this activity, students will work in teams of 3–4 to determine which materials and designs make a parachute that slows a weight's descent when it is dropped. When designing their parachutes, failure is an important teacher. Students will learn which materials and designs work best using trial and error. To build students' resilience, you might share that engineers must also first determine what fails to create the best designs.

Time: 10–25 minutes for building, plus testing time

Materials (available for students to choose from): various types of paper (tissue, printer, newspaper), fabric scraps or squares, plastic shopping bags, string, small weights such as 1-ounce fishing sinkers or small toys, rulers, hole punches, scissors, stepladder and stopwatch (for testing)

Instructions: Introduce the activity and share examples of real parachute designs to build students' background knowledge. Explain that teams will use the materials provided to create and test two to three parachute designs that slow the descent of a small weight or toy when dropped. Students will test their designs as they work to see if the parachutes open and slow the weights' descent, but they can only conduct tests from their own heights.

At the end of the build time, the teacher should drop students' parachutes from a stepladder. Students will time how long each drop takes. The more a parachute slows the descent of a weight, the better its design. During the final drop, students should look for what isn't working as desired (aka the failure) in their and other teams' designs. Identifying what and where the problem(s) are helps improve designs.

Make It Real

	Grades 3–7	Grades 8–12
• Each team creates only one parachute design. • Success is measured by whether the parachute opens and slows the weight's descent. If it doesn't, talk about what students might change to improve the design.	• Success is measured by how much the parachute slows the weight's descent. Talk about what students might change to improve the design.	• Teams conduct three trials for each design, making small adjustments to improve them after each drop. They can find the average drop time for each parachute design to determine which of their designs works best.

More for You: Ask your local fire department if the ladder truck is available to help with the parachute drop. Another option is to drop the parachutes down a stairwell in your school or off the school's roof if it is safe to do so.

Keep in Mind: The purpose of this activity is for students to test materials and try different designs. Remind students that they determined the best materials and designs for their parachutes by figuring out which didn't work. Failure helped them succeed.

Float Your Boat

When creating designs, engineers must test each design to failure to understand its limits. They need to know the maximum occupancy or maximum weight of a design to make sure it's safe for its intended use. Not knowing when a design will fail can be extremely dangerous. Students will work in pairs to build a boat that holds the most passengers possible using only the materials provided. Students then test their boat design by adding one passenger at a time until the boat fails and sinks.

Time: 10–25 minutes for building, plus testing time

Materials (available for students to choose from): Styrofoam blocks, cardboard, index cards, scissors, tape, pipe cleaners, wax paper, large bolts and large bucket or storage bin with water (for testing)

Instructions: Introduce the activity and show examples of boat designs. Make sure each pair gets one Styrofoam block and one piece of cardboard. Students can select from the other materials, but all pairs should have these same core pieces.

When building time is over, test one boat design at a time in a large bucket or bin of water. Begin placing bolts in the center of the boat and work outward to maintain consistency across trials. Keep track of how many passengers (bolts) each boat safely holds. A boat has failed once 50 percent of it is submerged. Discuss why students think some designs held more weight than others.

Make It Real

Grades PreK–2

- During testing, the teacher places the bolts on the boats. Keep track as a class of how many bolts each boat holds.

Grades 3–7

- During testing, the teacher places the bolts on the boats. Students track the number of bolts each boat holds using tally marks.

Grades 8–12

- Pairs take turns placing the bolts on their boats. They are responsible for tracking the number of passengers their boats hold and reporting this information to the class.

Keep in Mind: The point of this activity is not to determine which boat design holds the most passengers but, rather, to determine how many passengers each design can accommodate safely. Students need to test their boat to failure to determine its maximum occupancy.

Build a Bridge

To ensure people's safety, bridge engineers need to know under what conditions a bridge will fail, like how many cars the bridge deck can hold before it collapses. This information is crucial to a successful bridge design. In this activity, students will work in pairs to build a bridge using a truss, suspension, beam, or cable-stayed design. Each pair's bridge must sit on bridge abutments (created by the teacher) and span a given distance (determined by the teacher). Students then test which bridge design holds the most weight before collapsing.

Time: 10–25 minutes for building, plus testing time

Materials (available for students to choose from): straws, string, small paper clips, tape, scissors, small paper cups (1 per pair) and large bolts (for testing)

Instructions: Introduce the activity and show examples of truss, suspension, beam, and cable-stayed bridges. Encyclopædia Britannica's "bridge (engineering)" page has wonderful example images. Students can select one of these existing bridge designs or combine elements from different designs to create their bridges. Once building time is over, test the bridges one at a time. Set a bridge on the abutments, then place a small paper cup in the center and add one bolt at a time until the bridge collapses. Discuss what failures students encountered when building their bridges and what features make a successful bridge design.

Make It Real

- Consider having students at this grade level all make a flat bridge that crosses a narrow opening.

Grades 3–7

- Each pair predicts how many bolts their bridge will hold before breaking. Then they determine the actual number of bolts it holds.

Grades 8–12

- Students calculate the difference between the predicted weight and the actual weight their bridges hold.

- Students build the abutments for their bridges.

Keep in Mind: The shorter the distance bridges need to span, the easier this challenge is. Consider using a shorter span for younger grades; older grades should build bridges that span at least fifty centimeters.

Strongest Shapes

When students look at the world around them, they find shapes everywhere. From the circles of traffic lights and roundabouts to the triangles used in bridges and other structures to towering columns and pillars, shapes are an integral part of engineering, architecture, and design. In this activity, students will explore how shapes can create both strength and beauty. Younger students will work in pairs to explore the strength of various pillar shapes and determine which is the strongest. Older students will explore origami to see how shapes can be folded upon themselves to create three-dimensional designs.

Time: 10–20 minutes

Materials: (Grades PK–7): printer paper, tape, picture books or chapter books (for testing); **(Grades 8–12)** origami paper

Instructions: Introduce the activity and create a list of shapes with students. Where do they see these shapes in their everyday lives? Explain that shapes are an integral part of engineering, architecture, and design, but some shapes are stronger than others. Review how to fold paper to create various pillar shapes. Once folded, the shapes should look like paper columns. Students test the strength of their shapes by stacking one book at a time on the top of each column until it collapses. Have them record the number of books each shape successfully held. Discuss as a class what students noticed. Invite them to share their ideas for why some shapes make stronger pillars than others and why this information is important for engineers, builders, and designers. (In this activity, the circle column should be strongest since the weight is evenly distributed; shapes like triangles and squares collapse more easily since they support the weight on their edges and corners.)

Make It Real

Grades PK–2

- Encourage students to repeat a shape design to see if they can improve the results of their book test.

Grades 3–7

- If time permits, have students try to create paper origami boxes (find instructions online) and test how many books theirs hold before collapsing.

Grades 8–12

- Students watch the video in More for You and fold origami cranes instead of doing the main activity. Ask them what shapes they notice as they are folding their cranes. What failures do they experience?

- Students can make something else out of origami paper if they master the crane.

More for You: Origami Crane Folding Instructions, page 83

Share Aperture's video "Origami: The Art of Paper Folding" on YouTube, regardless of students' ages, to teach them more about how, through failure, art can be created (youtu.be/-Q6QZj02d qk).

Keep in Mind: Folding paper can be a difficult skill to learn, and students will likely experience some failure in folding their shapes or origami cranes. If you see students getting frustrated, help them take a step back to determine where they went wrong and try again.

Snake Charming

In this activity, students will work individually to test various materials to see which combinations create static electricity that can be used to "charm" tissue paper snakes. Students will need to use trial and error to figure out what materials (other than a balloon rubbed on someone's head) can create static electricity. Through trial-and-error experiences, students will learn that failing is a natural part of investigation. They will identify which materials work to charm their tissue paper snakes by ruling out the ones that don't.

Time: 10–25 minutes

Materials (available for students to choose from): tissue paper (1 piece per student), round tin pans (1 per student), scissors, markers, plastic rulers, wool fabric, construction paper, cotton socks, foam, plastic wrap, bubble wrap, cotton balls, silk scarves, nylon stockings

Instructions: Introduce the activity and show a video of a real snake charmer. Each student will do the following: Cut a spiral out of tissue paper to create a snake and, if time permits, decorate their snake. Place their snake in their tin pan. (See figure 1.1.) Rub various materials together, testing to see which combinations create static electricity by holding them over the snake until it starts to rise out of the pan.

Multiple combinations will create static electricity, but not all will. If a combination fails, encourage the student to try another they haven't yet tested. Once a student is successful at creating static electricity, see if they can use it to make their snake dance or perform tricks.

Make It Real

Grades PK–2	Grades 3–7	Grades 8–12
• Create a template for the snake to help students cut a spiral. Remind students that it is okay to make mistakes when cutting out their snakes. If they mess up, they can try again.	• Model how to cut the spiral snake out of the tissue paper. Encourage students to try other ways to cut out their snakes, especially if the way you modeled is not working.	• If time permits, allow students to explore other designs that they can charm or to try charming a snake made out of another material.

More for You: Students are creating an electrical charge by rubbing various materials together. Creating friction between materials causes an imbalance of positive and negative charges. The tissue paper snake is then attracted to the charged object and lifts out of the pan because it has an opposite charge.

Keep in Mind: Students will need to test various combinations of materials to figure out those that create enough static electricity to charm their tissue paper snakes. If students are stuck, help them come up with ideas for keeping track of what they've tried. They might need to test both materials over the snakes to determine which one became charged.

figure 1.1: tissue paper snake

This Side Up!

When packages are shipped, it's important to protect the items inside. Packing fragile items with protection can keep them from breaking. If an item is not packaged correctly and gets damaged in transit, the customer will want a refund. This is a failure for a business because they have lost that product and aren't able to profit from its sale. In this activity, students will work in teams of 2–3 to create a package to keep a fragile item (egg) from breaking during transit (when dropped).

Time: 10–25 minutes for building, plus testing time

Materials (available for students to choose from): hard-boiled eggs (1 per team), straws, paper cups, cotton balls, painter's tape, cupcake liners, pipe cleaners, scissors, stepladder (for testing)

Instructions: Introduce the activity. Tell teams that they can use any combination of materials to create their packages to protect their eggs. Once building time is over, test students' designs. Find an area outside to do the egg drop to make cleanup easier. The teacher drops students' designs from a stepladder. After the drop, students check their eggs for damage. Discuss why some designs failed while others were successful.

Make It Real

Grades K–2	Grades 3–7
• Teams can use as many materials as they would like to keep their eggs safe.	• Limit the amount of each material teams can use to keep their eggs safe.

Grades 8–12

- Price the materials and assign a budget. Teams must remain under budget when building the devices to keep their eggs safe.

- Consider dropping the eggs from three different heights. The eggs that survive the shortest fall move on to the next height, and so on until only a few eggs remain.

More for You: The science behind an egg drop centers around Sir Isaac Newton's three laws of motion. Students need to counteract the law that states that for every action there is an equal and opposite reaction. When the egg hits the ground, the ground applies a force onto the egg. Students need to use the materials to reduce the effect this force has on the egg when it makes impact.

Keep in Mind: The best way to figure out how to keep an egg safe in its package is to intentionally try to break it. We see this same concept in car design. Engineers intentionally crash cars with crash test dummies inside to determine which aspects of the car are dangerous to the dummy so they can make the car safer for human passengers.

Blast Off!

In this activity, students will work individually to design three straw rockets. All rockets will have the same body shape, but students will decide how many fins to add to each rocket and what fin shapes to use. Students will then test their rockets to determine which design travels the farthest. Students explore how many fins are needed on a rocket, including the placement of the fins, for a successful launch. Students will likely experience many failed launches while determining what works.

Time: 10–25 minutes for building, plus testing time (you may choose to spread this activity across two days: one for building and one for testing and improving rocket designs)

Materials (per student): 1 sheet of printer paper, scissors, wide straw, glue sticks, clear tape, 3–6 index cards, painter's tape and tape measure (for testing)

Instructions: Introduce the activity. Each student will do the following: To build the bodies for their rockets, cut their sheet of printer paper into three long strips that are of equal size. Wrap a paper strip (the long way) around their wide straw and glue or tape it closed to create a hollow tube that can easily slide off the straw. Then, fold over one end of the paper tube and secure it down using tape. This is the rocket's tip. Repeat for the other two strips. Next, create the rockets' fins. First draw the fins on the index cards, then cut them out and attach them to the rocket bodies. Students can use any number and shape of fins for their rockets, but they should change up their fin design for each model.

Set up an area where students can test their rockets, using a line of painter's tape as the starting point. Have them each place a rocket on the end of their straw, then blow into the straw to launch it. Measure how far each rocket travels.

Make It Real

- Students make only one rocket. After testing all the rockets, discuss why students think some rocket designs traveled farther than others. How might they improve their designs?

Grades 3–7

- Students each track the distance their rockets travel and consider why they got these various results. If any designs failed, ask students to consider what they might change to improve them.

Grades 8–12

- Provide time for each student to each improve their best design based on the test launch.

Keep in Mind: Many variables are at play when making and launching a rocket. NASA frequently has to call off rocket launches for things outside of their control, like bad weather or birds flying overhead. Students' rockets might not work for any number of reasons. Remind them that these failures are okay and that it is important to identify which rocket designs fail to determine which are most successful. Students can use this information to improve their designs.

Index Card Challenge

In this activity, students will work in teams of 3–4 to complete an index card challenge appropriate to their grade level. Students in grades PK–2 will build towers that can hold a book out of a given number of index cards. Students in grades 3–12 will cut their index cards to make a hollow ring and see what the largest object is that they can pass through a single index card. If failures happen, as they likely will, encourage students to change up their approach and try again.

Time: 20 minutes

Materials (per team): (Grades PK–2) index cards, heavy book; **(Grades 3–12)** index cards, scissors, classroom objects

Instructions: Introduce the activity. Give teams time to cut and test anir cards. Each team can cut their card however they choose, but they should not cut all the way through a card. If a team makes a wrong cut, cuts all the way through their card, or tears it, they can start again. Encourage teams to persist through mistakes and frustrations and try different strategies. At the end of time, have students demonstrate the largest objects that fit through their index cards without tearing them. *Note: Cutting index cards in this way will likely be too difficult for very young students; follow the instructions in Make It Real for grades PK–2 instead.*

Make It Real

Grades PK–2

- Have teams each build a tower that can hold the weight of one book out of a given number of index cards. As they build, teams can test their towers and make adjustments. At the end of the building time, see which team's tower is the tallest and can hold the book.

Grades 3–12

- If teams are struggling to figure out this challenge, offer a hint (see More for You). But try not to give away the whole solution; the point of this activity is for students to try and fail and try again using a different strategy.
- If teams are successful at fitting large objects through their cards, they can try to fit a human through them.

More for You: Here's how to cut an index card to fit a person through:

- Fold the card in half (the long way). Starting on the folded side, cut a slit most of the way through the card near each end (be sure not to cut all the way to the edge).
- Unfold the card, and cut the large middle section along the folded crease.
- Refold the card, and, starting on the unfolded edge (as close to the existing slit as you can, and not more than about one centimeter away), cut a slit going up toward the folded edge, without cutting through the edge.

- Flip the card over and cut another slit starting on the folded edge and going toward the unfolded edge.
- Continue cutting slits, alternating top and bottom, until the entire middle section is cut into an accordion.
- Open the card and see what you can fit through it.

Check out Sick Science!'s video "How to Step Through an Index Card - Sick Science! #054" for a demonstration (youtu.be/71bzxv0032s).

Keep in Mind: Students will likely fail in the process of building their towers or cutting their index cards to fit large objects through them. Encourage them to persist through frustrations and try different strategies. Ensure that students understand they can make mistakes and try again within the given time frame.

Balancing Act

In this activity, students will work individually to create an object they can balance on one finger. Students will have to practice balancing their objects on their fingers until they get the right placement and weight. It will take trial and error to get the objects to balance. Students need to learn from their failures to find success.

Time: 20 minutes

Materials (per student): scissors, straws, pipe cleaners, tape, wood beads, clay, crayons (grades PK–2)

Instructions: Introduce the activity. Talk about balance, using tightrope walkers as an example. Explain that tightrope walkers use a weighted pole to help lower their center of gravity, making it harder for them to topple when balancing above the ground. Tell students that they can get as creative as they'd like with the design for their objects. But like tightrope walkers, they will need to balance the weight on each side of their objects. When building time is up, students can discuss the failures they experienced and adjustments they made to get their objects to balance.

Make It Real

Grades PK–2

- Instead of building their own balancing objects, have each student decorate and cut out the robot in the Balancing Act Activity Sheet. Challenge them to first balance their robot on a finger. Once students are successful, invite them to try balancing their robots on a string tied between two chairs or desks.

Grades 3–7

- Challenge students to balance their objects on a string tied between two chairs or desks once they successfully balance them on a finger.

Grades 8–12

- Once students have mastered the balancing act with their objects, invite them to make their objects either heavier or longer. How does this change how the objects balance?

More for You: Balancing Act Activity Sheet, page 84

Keep in Mind: Students' objects will likely topple a few times before they figure out how to balance them. These failures help students make adjustments to find the right balance.

Skill 2: Creativity

Being creative isn't limited to making art. Creative people also generate ideas, solve problems, and create new and valuable things. Creativity can be tangible or intangible. Within STEAM, students use creativity when approaching problems—thinking outside the box and considering new ideas and solutions. In this way, STEAM provides students with the opportunity to be not just inventors but innovators.

The Role of the Teacher

The activities in this chapter encourage students who are reluctant to create. As young people get older, they tend to shy away from things that are challenging, especially if they perceive they aren't good at something. Students often group themselves as "creative" or "not creative." However, *everyone* can create. Your role is to guide students to understand that creativity isn't limited to being a "good" artist or painter or having work hung in a museum. Creating a video game, designing an app, making reflective clothing to keep people safe, taking a photo, writing a piece of fiction or nonfiction, cooking a dish, and planning a party are all examples of ways people can be creative.

Creativity as a STEAM Skill

Creativity is innate in all people. And it's not limited to being a good painter or potter. Someone can be creative as a chef, a writer, a musician, an engineer, or a scientist.

As you lead the strategies in this chapter, keep your ears and eyes open. Notice students who are struggling to see themselves as creative, and provide encouragement and motivation. Explicitly point out things they've done or ideas they've had that are creative, and celebrate their creative solutions and problem-solving abilities. Here are some more things you can do to support creativity in your classroom.

Set up a space with supplies and materials where students can freely create. When supplying materials, give students plenty of options to choose from. This doesn't mean you need to spend a lot of money. A trip to the dollar store or the grocery store, or a call to your school community, will yield more than enough interesting materials. Encourage students to see and use items in new ways.

Celebrate creativity with examples of things other people have created. Prototype sketches and engineering blueprints are great ways to showcase the creativity that goes into STEAM careers, while displaying student-made objects and student-generated ideas highlights and encourages young people's creativity.

Provide time for students to work on passion projects. For many students, a lack of time, space, and materials to pursue what they're interested in can limit creative thinking in their learning. By removing (many of) the barriers for what students learn and how they show their learning, you foster a learning environment where great things can happen.

Find interdisciplinary opportunities. Collaborate with your school's art teacher to brainstorm ways to implement creative art opportunities in your projects. Encourage students to keep a journal or notebook to record their thoughts and ideas. Include movement, music, and visual media as options for students to show their learning and thinking.

Marble Maze

Mazes, like other puzzles, require students to solve a problem creatively. Designing a maze for others to solve also requires creativity. In this activity, each student will create a marble maze. Students will need to identify start and end points for their mazes, but the rest of the design is up to them. Encourage them to get creative, adding dead ends, junctions, and other obstacles to increase the difficulty of their mazes.

Time: 10–25 minutes

Materials (per student): paper plate or shoebox, marble, plastic straws, tape, scissors, marker

Instructions: Introduce the activity and show a few examples of mazes. Each student should first draw their maze design on their plate or inside their shoebox. Then they cut straws to make the maze walls and tape them in place. Once their maze is finished, they can guide a marble through by tipping the plate or shoebox. Remind students never to put marbles in their noses or mouths.

Make It Real

Grades PreK–2	Grades 3–7	Grades 8–12
• Small marbles may be a choking hazard for very young students. Consider using large marbles instead.	• Give students the marbles at the start of the activity and allow them to test and improve their designs within the time frame.	• Have students swap their mazes with partners to see if they can solve each other's mazes.

Keep in Mind: As long as students' mazes have start and end points, there is no wrong way to complete this activity. This makes it an excellent opportunity for students to practice their creative problem-solving skills.

Solar Prints

Wait for a sunny day to do this activity! Each student will use various items and sunlight to create a solar print art piece. Students can get as creative as they'd like with their solar print designs, experimenting with different exposure times, objects, and object placements to accomplish their desired prints.

Time: 20 minutes for design creation, plus exposure time

Materials (available for students to choose from): various colors of dark-toned construction paper or solar print paper or fabric, small rocks or weights, various items from nature, sunlight

Instructions: Locate a space outdoors in direct sunlight that does not experience a lot of foot traffic, since students' prints will need to sit outside for several hours without being disturbed. It's best to start this activity early in the day.

Introduce the activity. Have students set up their papers outdoors, using small rocks or weights to keep them from blowing away. These weights will sit on the prints for the full exposure time, so students should think about how and whether to incorporate them into their designs. Students should set objects on their papers to create their designs and weigh the objects down as needed. Leave the papers outside in the sun for several hours to create the prints. Explain that the longer the papers sit in the sunlight, the more contrast the prints will have. Students may want to remove objects at different points during the day to get a desired look. They can finish their designs by adding other materials or media. Display the artwork.

Make It Real

- Have students pick only two or three objects to place on their papers.

Grades 3–7

- Consider having students select objects to create a scene for their designs.

Grades 8–12

- Try doing this activity using solar print paper or fabric. Encourage students to incorporate some objects that are more detailed than others into their designs. They might even want to try layering objects or removing or adding new objects throughout the day.

Keep in Mind: This strategy focuses on students' creativity, but it also includes some trial and error. Often, artists and engineers make multiple attempts before getting a design or piece of artwork the way they want it. During the design process, have the students consider changing the placement of their items, focusing on creativity, to achieve their desired designs. Small changes can help improve a design.

Tactile Paints

Each student will make a set of puff paints and use them to create a piece of artwork. Once dried, the paints provide a tactile experience, where students can both see and feel their art. Older students can explore these tactile paints as well, using them to add dimension to artwork or multimedia creations.

Time: 20 minutes for painting, plus overnight drying time

Materials: construction paper (2 pieces per student); pencils; unscented shaving cream (not gel based); Elmer's liquid school glue; paper bowls (1 per student); a few ¼-cup measuring cups; food coloring; cups, plastic spoons, paintbrushes or craft sticks (4 of each per student)

Instructions: Introduce the activity and show a sample art piece you created with tactile paints. Each student will do the following: First, draw a design for their artwork on construction paper. Then, mix ¼ cup of glue and ¼ cup of shaving cream in a paper bowl. Divide the shaving-cream mixture into their four cups and stir in 2–3 drops of food coloring per cup to create different colors of paint. Once their paints are mixed, fill in the design they created.

Make It Real

Grades PreK–2

- You may want to add the food coloring to students' paints to avoid waste.

Grades 3–7

- Allow students to make custom colors.

Grades 8–12

- Let students use other materials for their art pieces beyond what is listed. Encourage them to get creative.

More for You: The tactile paints become puffy because the shaving cream evaporates over time, creating air pockets under the dried glue.

Keep in Mind: Most students have had experience painting in art class or at home. Typically, those paints are one dimensional and provide no tactile experience once dried. Tactile art encourages the viewer to touch the art as part of the experience.

Builders Showcase

In this activity, students will work individually to use their creativity to design a building or structure that can be shared with their classmates during a Builders Showcase. Students can use any materials for this project, so encourage them to be as creative as possible. During the showcase, invite family and friends to tour students' structures.

Time: multi-day project

Materials (recommended): recyclable materials, art supplies

Instructions: Introduce the activity. Students will need multiple days to build their structures. They can build at home or at school. Encourage them to get creative with the materials they use. Students display and share their structures in a Builders Showcase, celebrating their and classmates' creativity.

Make It Real

- Students each choose one structure to build: a house, an apartment, a school, a store, or a library. They can look at images of their structures for inspiration but should create their own original designs.
- When students present their buildings, they share what they made and how.

Grades 3–7

- Students each select a famous structure from around the world to research and build. They should make their structures look as close to the real ones as possible.
- When students present their buildings, they share the locations of the real buildings, why they're important structures, and the materials they used to re-create them.

Grades 8–12

- Students each build a futuristic version of a common structure using an original design.
- When students present their designs, they share what they made, how they made them, and what makes their designs futuristic.

Keep in Mind: Students create their buildings using materials of their choice. This allows them to choose not only what they create but also how they will use their materials to create them. Having voice and choice in this creative project can be a major motivating factor and increase engagement.

Invention Convention

In this activity, students will work individually to design an invention that solves a problem they or someone they know has and create a prototype of the invention. They can use any materials and should be as creative as possible. They share their designs during an Invention Convention. You may also want to invite family and friends to view the inventions students create.

Time: multi-day project

Materials (recommended): recyclable materials, art supplies

Instructions: Introduce the activity and share some examples of inventions and prototypes students have created in the past, if possible. Students will need multiple days to design their inventions and build their prototypes. Prototypes do not have to function. Students can build at home or at school. They should take some time to brainstorm their inventions and what problems the inventions solve before building their prototypes. They can also research inventions that solve similar problems. Inventions should be students' original designs and not something that has already been created. At the Invention Convention, students present the inventions they created, discussing what they made and the problems their inventions solve.

Make It Real

Grades PK–2

- Each student creates an invention that solves a problem they have.

Grades 3–7

- Each student creates an invention that solves a problem someone else in their family or class has.

Grades 8–12

- Each student creates an invention that solves a problem in their community.
- Challenge students to try building working prototypes.

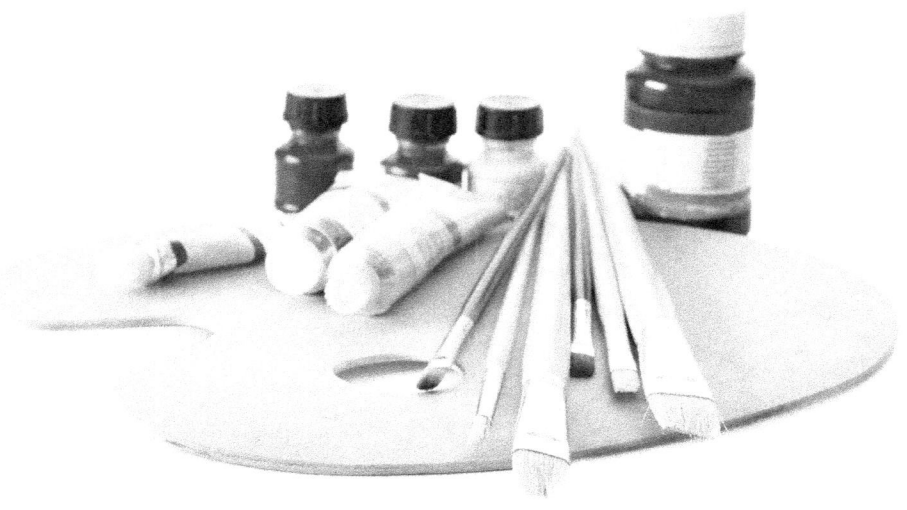

More for You: It can help to start this activity by having students answer the following questions. Depending on their age, they can either answer the questions themselves or interview someone else to help narrow down a problem to be solved.

- Can you name two or three problems you have at home, school, or in your community?
- How could these problems be solved?
- How do they impact your life or someone else's life?
- What do you hope would be improved by solving them?

Keep in Mind: Remind students that a problem does not have to be "big." It could be as simple as keeping a pencil from rolling off a desk and falling on the ground. The ability to view themselves as inventors who find creative solutions to problems can be a major motivating factor and increase engagement.

Rainbow Designs

In this activity, students will work individually to explore how colors can be combined to create new colors through the creation of rainbow designs. Students in grades PK–2 will explore colors by creating rainbow butterflies. Students in grades 3–7 will explore colors by creating suncatchers. If you choose to do a color activity with students in grades 8–12, they may enjoy tie-dyeing.

Time: 20–40 minutes, plus drying time

Materials (per student):
(Grades PK–2) white coffee filter, tray, washable markers, eye dropper or small spoon, shallow bowl of water, pipe cleaner

(Grades 3–7) flexible plastic lid, Elmer's liquid school glue, food coloring, toothpick, hole punch, 1-foot piece of string

Instructions: (Grades PK–2) Introduce the activity. Have students set their coffee filters on their trays to keep the color from bleeding onto the surface below. Each student will do the following: Flatten the coffee filter and use markers to color a design on it. Using either an eye dropper or a small spoon, drip water onto their colored coffee filter until it is wet but not oversaturated. Place the tray aside to dry. Once the coffee filter is dry, pinch it in the middle and wrap it with a pipe cleaner. (Students can also accordion-fold the filters before pinching.) Keep the ends of the pipe cleaner loose and curl them to make butterfly antennae.

(Grades 3–7) Introduce the activity. Each student will do the following: Put their lid on their desk with the lip facing up. Pour glue into the lid to cover the surface. Put a few drops of food coloring (in different colors) on the glue, then swirl the colors using a toothpick. Let the glue dry on the lid for a couple of days. When the glue design is fully dried, remove it from the lid and use a hole punch to make a hole at the top, then thread with string. Students can hang their suncatchers in a window.

Make It Real

- Encourage students to pay attention to how the colors are mixed in each design before creating their next butterflies.

- Talk to students about how the three primary colors can be mixed to make other colors. Have students point out on their finished butterflies where that occurred.

Grades 3–7

- Encourage students to slowly mix the colors in the glue, paying attention to the designs they are creating.

- If students bring in more than one lid, allow them to make two suncatchers. Encourage them to explore different color combinations in each.

Grades 8–12

- Have older students explore color through tie-dyeing white bandanas (1 per student). Tie-Dye Party kits are useful for this activity. Students can use either a traditional rubber-band method or paint on the dye using paintbrushes.

Keep in Mind: How colors are mixed to create other colors as well as the rules and guidelines for color schemes are all part of color theory. Students in grades PK–2 typically learn about primary colors, students in grades 3–7 learn about secondary colors, and grades 8 and up learn about tertiary colors. The use of a color wheel can help students at all grade levels understand and further explore color theory.

Tessellations

A tessellation is a repeating pattern created by tracing a shape so there are no gaps through reflection, translation, and rotation. In this activity, each student will create a tessellation. Tessellations are a great way to connect mathematics, science, and art in a single activity. And it's fun for students of all ages!

Time: 20–40 minutes

Materials (per student): (Grades PK–7) blank paper, drawing materials, tangram blocks; **(Grades 8–12)** square sticky note, pencil, tape, scissors, blank paper

Instructions: Introduce the activity and share a couple examples of tessellations you've created. Students will make their tessellations by tracing a chosen shape on paper. Once students have traced their shapes once, they line up their templates with one edge of the tracing on their papers and trace the remaining sides. By doing so, they create repeating patterns that have no gap between shapes. Students continue to trace their shapes as many times as directed or until they've filled their papers. Once students have completed their tessellations, let them color their creations. Then share them with the class, celebrating students' creativity.

Make It Real

Grades PK–2

- Students each pick one shape to use in their tessellation. You might have them trace their shape only four to six times before decorating.

Grades 3–7

- Students each pick two to three shapes that they'll use. Explain that all shapes do not have to be the same size, but each same shape should be.

Grades 8–12

- Students each create their own shapes for their tessellation (see page 78).

More for You: Tessellations (Grades 8–12), page 78

Keep in Mind: Tessellation art requires that no gaps exist between shapes. Students can create their tessellations with one shape or try combining different shapes and sizes to create their visual art pieces. Encourage them to get creative, rotating and reflecting shapes to create new designs.

Mini Movies

In this activity, each student will create their own mini movie using a series of still pictures. Students in grades PK–7 will create flip-books, while students in grades 8–12 will create zoetropes. Flip-books and zoetropes are types of animation that existed before film. Both work on the principle that our brains fill in the motion between still images, creating an illusion of a moving picture.

Time: 30–60 minutes

Materials (per student): 20–30 dot stickers (grades PK–2), 10–15 index cards cut in half, pencil

Instructions: Prepare blank flip-books by cutting index cards in half and stapling them together. Introduce the activity and show an example of a flip-book you created. Consider modeling how to make a sequence using dot stickers or simple stick person drawings. Once students have filled the books with their sequences, show them how to flip the pages to watch their dots or pictures move. If time permits, they can flip the books over and create new animations.

Make It Real

- Give each student 20–30 dot stickers of the same color. Students put one sticker on each page of their books, in a different place on each page. Students can draw faces on the dots, changing the expression on each page, or add arms and legs.

Grades 3–7

- Students should draw the character in their flip-books, making the character do something slightly different on each page.
- After students test their flip-books, they can make changes to illustrations as needed.

Grades 8–12

- Students at this grade level may enjoy creating zoetropes (see page 79) instead to increase the challenge of the activity.

More for You: Zoetropes, page 79

Keep in Mind: For the motion to look seamless in both the flip-books and the zoetropes, students need to sequence their animations. Consider modeling how to do this or sharing an example.

Kaleidoscopes

In this activity, each student will create a kaleidoscope that changes designs when rotated. Sir David Brewster invented the kaleidoscope in 1816. The name kaleidoscope comes from the Greek words *kalos* for "beautiful," *eidos* for "form," and *skopein* meaning "to look or see." Each student draws four to six patterns on a disc that are reflected off the mirrored surfaces of a prism, changing as the disc moves. Students tap into their creativity when drawing their patterns, using different combinations of shapes and colors. As they rotate their kaleidoscopes, the mirrored prisms create new designs out of their patterns. *Note that this activity is intended for students in grades PK–7 and may be too simple for older grades.*

Time: 45 minutes, in two sessions for younger grades

Materials: 6-inch-long cardboard tubes (1 per student), Circle Templates (1 per student, printed on cardstock), Mylar sheets or self-stick mirror sheets, scissors, tape, straws, markers

Instructions: Introduce the activity and show a sample kaleidoscope you created. Each student will do the following: Cut the Mylar or mirror sheets into skinny rectangles the length of their tube (width will vary depending on the size of the tube). Each tube will need three pieces that, when taped together, create a triangular prism as long as the tube that fits snugly inside it. After cutting their rectangular mirror pieces, they create their prism. Line up the three pieces side by side (the long way) and tape them together. Then attach the two ends together to make a prism with the mirrored surface facing in, and slide the prism inside the cardboard tube. Next, tape the straw along the tube so that part of it extends about half an inch beyond the end of the tube. Then decorate their circle in different patterns and cut it out. Poke a hole in the center of the circle with a pencil. Slide the circle on the straw with the drawings facing the mirrored tube. Figure 2.1 shows a completed kaleidoscope.

Direct students to look through the ends of their tubes that don't have the paper circles on them and slowly spin the circles, watching as the designs change. Invite them to share their kaleidoscopes with each other.

Make It Real

- Encourage students to decorate each part of their circles differently. The more creative they are with their patterns and colors, the more exciting their kaleidoscope images will be.

More for You: Circle Template, page 85

Keep in Mind: Students' kaleidoscopes work similarly to a real one, but not exactly. As light reflects off the mirrored sheets inside students' tubes, that light travels to the other surfaces, causing a reflection of a reflection. As students rotate the discs they created, the designs shift and change, creating new visuals.

figure 2.1: kaleidoscope

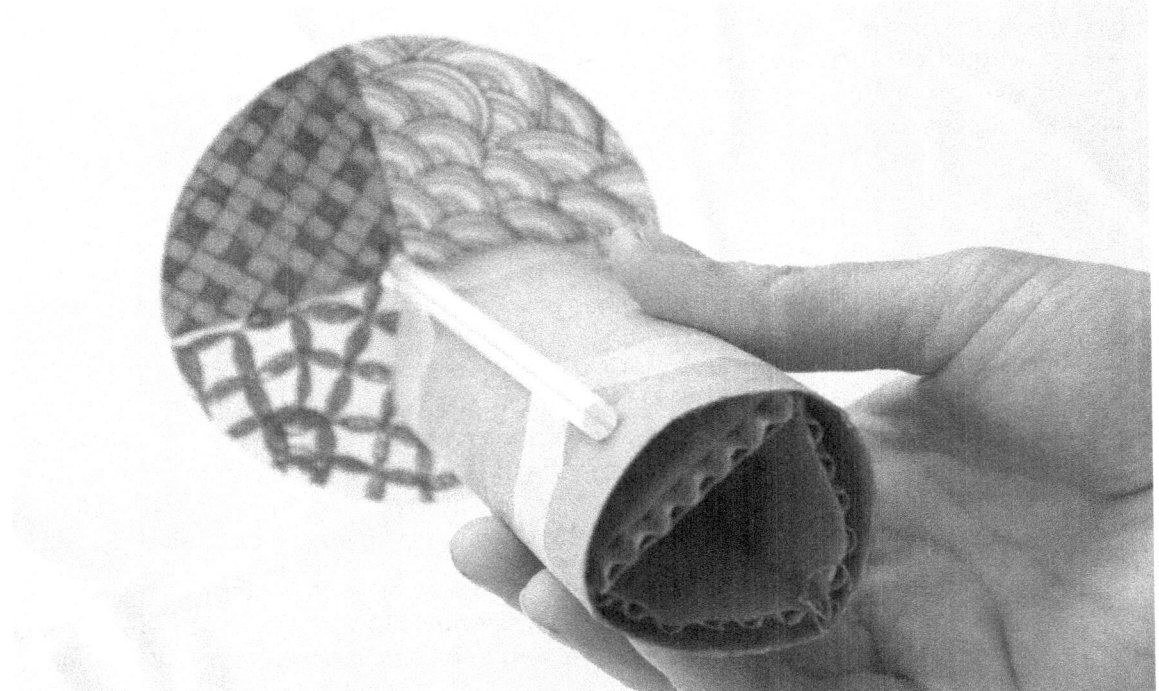

Paper Marbling

In this activity, each student will create marbled paper art using food dye and shaving cream. This is a less messy alternative to more traditional paper-marbling methods and has a quicker drying time. Encourage students to get creative with their designs and how they might display them. They can create cards, wall art, or something else.

Time: 20–30 minutes for painting, plus drying time

Materials: unscented shaving cream (not gel based), round tin pans (1 per student), food coloring, toothpicks, 5-x-7-inch white cardstock (a few pieces per student), craft sticks

Instructions: Introduce the activity. Give each student a tin pan with some shaving cream. Students can choose 2–3 colors of food coloring for their designs. Each student will do the following: Drop food coloring onto the shaving cream in their pan and use their toothpick to create their marbled design. Once a student has the design they want, they lay a piece of paper on top of their marbled shaving cream, give the paper a few taps, and peel it off. Then they use a craft stick to scrape off any extra shaving cream and reveal their design.

Students put their marbled prints aside to dry. As time permits, invite students to make more prints. A student might try to make a new print with the same batch of shaving cream, can add an additional color to their design and make a new print, or can empty their pan and start over with an entirely new design.

Make It Real

- At this age level, you may want to control the food coloring to cut back on waste.
- Model how to use a toothpick to swirl the colors on the shaving cream into a design.

Grades 3–12

- Have students research and try other marbling applications at home, then bring in their artwork to share with the class.

Keep in Mind: Though the main focus of this strategy is on students' creativity, it also encourages students to use trial and error to see which color combinations and swirl patterns create the best designs. Not every print they make is going to turn out as well as others. Encourage students to pay close attention to what they liked and didn't like about each print. This will help them adjust their creative processes on subsequent prints.

Skill 3: Communication

Communication is crucial to building relationships and connecting with others. At its core, communication is the ability to convey information to others. In STEAM, it means you share your ideas, spread awareness about your work, and engage in constructive debate to solve problems.

The Role of the Teacher

The strategies in this chapter help students articulate their ideas and solutions to problems. You can encourage students to take notes and capture their thinking in words, pictures, or numbers. Provide opportunities for students to engage in discourse that requires them to debate and defend their claims with evidence and reasoning. You can facilitate debate by encouraging students to consider opposing viewpoints and approach arguments and the STEAM strategies with an empathetic lens.

Communication as a STEAM Skill

Whether students pursue a career in STEAM or not, having strong communication skills is important in jobs and in life. Being a good communicator means you effectively share your ideas and information with others. But communication is not exclusive to talking. Being a skilled and active listener who pays attention and asks questions is equally important. Here are some ideas to build students' communication skills as you work through the STEAM strategies in this section.

Provide each student with a notebook to capture their ideas, research, notes, claims, and evidence. Students can also practice writing formally and informally about different topics. Can they write a letter to a younger person explaining their ideas? What about a letter to a science magazine or newspaper?

Establish ways to be an active listener and take turns while talking. There are many frameworks and protocols for productive discussion and debate. Take time to practice the basics of discussion using low-stakes issues before discussing bigger issues. Making sure students understand the rules (and the intent of the rules) helps them learn to listen and understand even when they don't agree.

Give students space to understand their emotions. Encourage students to engage in introspection, examining their own feelings and reactions to what others say. The more time students spend thinking about what and why they want to communicate, the clearer they will be.

Allow for many paths to share. Students may feel most comfortable communicating by making videos, creating visuals, writing poems, or giving speeches. Show examples of STEAM communicators who use a variety of media to share their ideas.

- Dr. Stephen Hawking, a theoretical physicist, used assistive technology, including a thumb switch and a blink-switch attached to his glasses, to control his computer and communicate.
- Mae Jemison is an engineer, physician, and former astronaut for NASA. She is also the first African American woman to travel to space, as well as a published author of both children's books and an autobiography.
- Katherine Johnson was a mathematician whose calculations of orbital mechanics helped NASA with space flights, including the 1962 moon landing. She authored "Notes on Space Technology" and multiple lectures.
- Jimmy Chin is a *National Geographic* photographer and filmmaker who captured Alex Honnold's rock climbing in the film *Free Solo*. He is also a mountaineer himself.

STEAM Challenge

Host a STEAM Challenge with your class, or even with the entire school. Here are a few challenge ideas: create something to help carry Halloween candy, create a board game, create something that moves, make a musical instrument, create a piece of 3D art using only paper products. The sky is the limit! Once you've set the challenge, students will work in small groups or individually to create and build something that meets the challenge, using everyday items in their homes or recyclable goods. Students then use verbal or written communication to present what they made with the larger group.

Time: 1 week to 1 month, depending on whether you choose to do the STEAM Challenge as a classroom activity or an at-home project

Materials: recyclable materials, art supplies

Instructions: Introduce the activity. Each student must create an item to complete the STEAM Challenge determined by the teacher. Stress that students should use everyday items or recyclable goods to build their creations. Students can get help from adults but should do most of the work themselves. While students do need to meet the challenge brief, make sure you keep the brief open-ended, allowing for creativity. There is no right or wrong way to complete a challenge. At the end of the project, students present their creations, practicing communication skills.

Make It Real

Grades PK–2

- Provide sentence stems to help students communicate what they created.

Grades 3–7

- Set aside time for students to practice presenting their creations.

Grades 8–12

- Set up a recording booth with a video camera or laptop to record student presentations. Share presentations on the school website or social media (with approval).

More for You: You might choose to do this strategy as a monthly STEAM Challenge that students complete at home. If so, share the new challenge on the first day of each month, and have students turn projects in at the end of the month.

Keep in Mind: There is no right or wrong way for students to complete a STEAM Challenge, and students can get as creative as they'd like. The STEAM Challenge is also an opportunity to practice communicating—to talk about what they created and share their ideas.

Bubble Wands

In this activity, students will individually test various designs for a bubble wand and make an argument for which design makes the best bubbles. Encourage students to try different geometric shapes when making their wands, documenting which produced the best bubbles. Students write or discuss why they believe the wand shapes they chose are the best. You'll want to wait for nice weather to do this activity since bubbles can be messy indoors.

Time: 1 class period or instructional block

Materials (for students to choose from): pipe cleaners, tangram blocks (grades PK–2), scissors, pony beads, bubble solution, shallow pans

Instructions: Introduce the activity. Discuss as a class what makes a bubble great. You may want to share an example or do a demo for younger grades. Have each student use the materials provided to create their bubble wand. They can use the pony beads to stabilize (and decorate) their bubble wand's handle. Encourage students to test different shapes to determine which shape makes the best bubbles. At the end of the activity, students share what shapes they think made the best bubbles and why.

Make It Real

- Have students work in pairs, and provide tangram blocks to help them make their wand shapes. They can wrap a pipe cleaner around the edges of the tangram block to create a hollow shape.
- Allow students to verbally share why their bubble wand designs made the best bubbles.

Grades 3–7

- Give students time to write an argument for why their bubble wand designs are the best.
- Students debate which shape makes the best wand design.

Grades 8–12

- Encourage students to try creating 3D shapes for their wands.
- Have students write a CER (claim, evidence, reasoning) for why their bubble wand designs are the best, and conduct a class debate about the designs.

More for You: Though you can buy it, bubble solution is very easy to make. Just mix 1 cup of water, 2 tablespoons of light corn syrup, and 4 tablespoons of dishwashing liquid until everything is dissolved.

Keep in Mind: Some shapes are better than others for blowing bubbles, but this activity is not about students choosing the correct shape. Rather, it's about their ability to argue and defend their choices. Students should be able to communicate claims about which bubble wand shape is the best. They will use evidence from their trials to support why a given shape worked better as a bubble wand design than others.

Lava Lamps

In this activity, each student will create a lava lamp, following along as you demonstrate the process. They then create step-by-step instructions for someone else. While there isn't an element of creativity in this activity, students typically love it. It shows cause and effect and how matter changes. Listening to and following procedural steps also helps students become better communicators.

Time: 10–30 minutes

Materials (per student): empty clear plastic bottle with cap, funnel, vegetable oil, water, food coloring, Alka-Seltzer tablet (broken into at least 4 pieces)

Instructions: Introduce the activity. Each student will do the following: Using a funnel, fill their bottle three-quarters full with vegetable oil. (You may want to mark a fill line on the bottles for younger grades.) Then they add water to fill the bottle the rest of the way. Finally, they add three drops of food coloring to their bottle. Now, pass out the Alka-Seltzer tablets. Remind students not to put tablets in their mouths for any reason. Each student breaks a tablet into at least four pieces, puts one piece of the tablet into their bottle, and puts the cap on. They should not put the entire tablet in at once. Students can create their step-by-step instructions as they build their lava lamps or all at once after they've finished the entire project.

Make It Real

Grades PK–2	Grades 3–7	Grades 8–12
• Students draw pictures of the steps they took to make their lava lamps.	• Students draw and write what they did for each step. You might provide a word bank for this activity.	• Students draw pictures and write procedural steps after completing the entire project.

More for You: Have you ever heard the expression "oil and water do not mix"? This is because water molecules are polar and oil molecules are nonpolar. The polar molecules in water are attracted to other polar molecules, while the nonpolar molecules in oil are attracted to other nonpolar molecules. These different polarities make water and oil unable to mix. The different densities of water and oil are why, before students add the Alka-Seltzer to their lava lamps, the less-dense oil sits on top of the denser water. When students add the tablets, they will sink through the oil to the water at the bottom of the bottles. Once Alka-Seltzer hits water, it fizzes, creating carbon dioxide bubbles. These lighter gas bubbles rise to the surface, pulling along some colored water and giving the appearance of globs of liquid rising and falling, like in a lava lamp.

Keep in Mind: The point of this activity is communication. Being a good listener is an important part of being a strong communicator. In this activity, students practice their communication skills by creating procedural directions for someone else to follow. Students need to both follow the directions to create their own lamps and relay those steps to someone else.

Cloud in a Jar

Meteorologists are STEAM professionals who study the atmosphere and how it affects the environment. They use this information to predict the weather and trends in climate. In this activity, students become meteorologists. They'll first each create a cloud in a jar and then use it as a prop for conducting their own weather report. Students can either write or orally report about the weather occurring in their jars. Communicating and delivering a message is a key part of a meteorologist's job.

Time: 30 minutes

Materials (per student): plastic jar, water, shaving cream (not gel based), food coloring

Instructions: Introduce the activity. Each student will do the following: Fill their jar three-quarters full with water. (You may want to mark the jars with a fill line for younger grades.) Then add shaving cream to the top of the water like a cloud. Drop 3–6 drops of food coloring on top of the rain cloud. Observe their shaving-cream cloud in their jar and see what happens to the food coloring (the drops should come out the bottom of the cloud and drop like rain into the water). Finally, they develop a weather report about the observation. Allow time for students to give their weather reports to partners or in front of the whole class.

Make It Real

- Consider reading *It Looked Like Spilt Milk* and talk about clouds and cloud shapes. Take students outside to look at clouds.

Grades 3–7	Grades 8–12
• Consider reading *This Book Is Made of Clouds*. Discuss and review the phases of the water cycle. Ask students to identify which phase of the water cycle their clouds represent.	• Have students create more complex clouds in a jar (see page 80). • Have students record their weather reports and play them for the class. If your school has a green screen, this is a great time to use it.

More for You: Cloud in a Jar (Grades 8–12), page 80

Keep in Mind: Meteorologists must communicate complex topics in a short amount of time to broad audiences. They often write and deliver weather reports after conducting research about the forecast. Being an effective communicator helps them engage the public to share this important information. Having the students give a weather report about their clouds helps them practice sharing information.

Mirror Me

In this activity, students will work in pairs to mirror a design. One student (Student A) will use various materials to create a design or structure behind a privacy shield. Then they will explain to their partner (Student B) how to create what they made, without showing them. The goal is for Student A to communicate to Student B how to mirror (replicate) what they created.

Time: 20 minutes

Materials (per pair): 2 privacy shields (such as folders or binders), 2 sets of the same materials (classroom items and art supplies)

Instructions: Introduce the activity. Explain that students will work as partners using the same materials to create the same thing without being able to see what the other person is doing. Designate one student in each pair as Student A and the other as Student B. Student A will create a design behind the privacy of their shield and communicate how to make the design to Student B. Then both students reveal their designs to see how well they communicated. Have pairs take apart their designs and repeat the activity, with Student B as the designer and Student A the listener. Talk about the challenges students experienced in communicating about the designs.

Make It Real

Grades PK-2

- Give students few items to use in their designs.
- Student A can describe what they are doing as they create so Student B can follow along at the same time.

Grades 3–7

- Student A will create their full design, then describe it as Student B tries to re-create the design.

Grades 8–12

- Have students give written instructions instead of verbal ones.

More for You: Building blocks such as DUPLO bricks are a great material for this activity.

Keep in Mind: If students pick too many materials, it may be difficult to communicate directions for mirroring the design. If they're having difficulty communicating, remind them that scaling back the number of materials can help.

Brush Bots

In this activity, students will create robot characters using toothbrush heads and a few other craft items. Once they've finished decorating their brush bots, they each write a creative story about their bot. Creative writing is a wonderful way for students to practice written communication. You can also extend the learning and fun by adding materials to make the brush bots move!

Time: 30–45 minutes

Materials (per student): toothbrush head (with handle cut off), pom poms, small dot stickers, googly eyes; **additional materials for making brush bots move:** coin battery (CR2032), double-sided foam sticker, pager motor, wire cutter, wire stripper

Instructions: Introduce the activity and show a sample brush bot character you created. Invite students to decorate their toothbrush heads using the pom poms, googly eyes, and stickers to create their bots. After playing with their brush bots for a while, students write creative stories about them and share their stories with partners or the entire class.

Make It Real

	Grades 3–7	Grades 8–12
• Have each student draw or write a short story about their brush bot. Provide a few ideas for the setting (school, park, home) and sentence stems.	• Have each student write a short story about their brush bot. They should include a problem that the brush bot needs to solve.	• Have each student write a short story or draw a comic strip about their brush bot.

More for You: If you'd like students to make brush bots that move, you'll have to purchase a few extra items (see Materials). The video "How to Build a Bristlebot: Build Guide" by Brown Dog Gadgets on YouTube (youtu.be/oe10JCItP6Q) is a good example, showing how adding a few common materials can give students' brush bots life. Doing this activity with moving bots gives students exposure to different materials and shows how something designed to do one thing can be used to do something else.

Keep in Mind: Each student's brush bot will be unique. The story they write should be just as creative. Encourage students to think about a day in the life of their brush bots or what adventure their bots might be on. You may even provide graphic organizers to help students with their writing. If time permits, invite students to share their creative short stories.

Worm Overboard!

In this activity, students will work in teams of 3–4 to save a worm that has fallen overboard. Explain that the worm was sitting in his boat when it tipped over. The worm had forgotten to put on his life jacket before getting in the boat. Luckily, each boat comes with a life preserver ring. Working as a team, students will need to get the life preserver around the worm first, then flip the boat over and put the worm back inside, without harming the worm. Students can use only the materials provided; can never touch the worm, boat, or life preserver with their hands; and must keep the worm safe from danger. Once a team successfully saves their worm, they can help verbally coach another team, practicing communication skills.

Time: 10–25 minutes

Materials (per team): sheet of blue paper, small cup, gummy worm, gummy ring candy that can stretch, paper clips (1–2 per student), 1-foot pieces of yarn (1 per student)

Instructions: Introduce the activity and have each team tip their boat (paper cup), spilling their worm and gummy candy into the water (sheet of blue paper). Team members must work together and communicate to right their boat and save their worm. Once a team successfully completes the challenge, they should put their tools in the boat with the worm. Then, they can help a team still trying to save their worm by verbally coaching them. They are not allowed to touch other teams' tools or worms.

Make It Real

Grades PK–2

- Each student gets two paper clips and one piece of yarn as tools to help save the worm.

Grades 3–7

- Each student gets one paper clip and one piece of yarn as tools to help save the worm.

Grades 8–12

- Each student gets one paper clip as a tool to help save the worm.
- To increase difficulty, allow students to use only one hand during this challenge.

More for You: While there are many strategies that work for saving the worm, stabbing the life preserver or the worm with the paper clip to move them does not count. If someone tries this, they will need to start over with a strategy that does not harm their worm or life preserver.

Keep in Mind: To be successful in this activity, *every* team must save their worm. Students will need to work within their teams and with members of other teams to ensure all the worms in the room are saved. Students' verbal communication is, therefore, key. Notice if teams are having difficulty communicating and offer support.

Maze Walker

In this activity, students will work in teams of 3–4 to program a robot (student) to walk a maze. You can increase the challenge for older students by asking them to pick up objects and place them in buckets before exiting the maze. Students take turns acting as the robot and the programmers. Robots must follow the programmers' commands, even if they are incorrect. Programmers and robots cannot speak to one another. They can only communicate through a special programming language.

Time: 20–40 minutes

Materials (per team): painter's tape; 3–4 small objects; 3–4 buckets or large bowls; dry-erase board, marker, and eraser

Instructions: Prepare one maze per team by taping a path along the floor. Make sure each maze has a start and an end. To add difficulty, consider adding items that robots will need to pick up and drop in buckets before exiting the maze.

Introduce the activity, explaining that each team will need to use a programming language to move their robot. The programming language students should use consists of arrows pointing in the direction they want the robot student to move, a check mark meaning pick up an object, a star meaning drop an object in the bucket, and an X meaning stop. Model how to draw commands and move through the maze. For example, to get a student to turn right and move forward one space, draw a right arrow and a forward arrow ($\longrightarrow$ $\uparrow$). Have students take turns being the robot and the programmers.

Make It Real

- Encourage students to practice left and right when giving directions in addition to the directional arrows.

- For younger students, omit the objects and buckets and just have students navigate the mazes.

- If students are struggling to draw arrows, you can print off directional arrows for them to use or have them give verbal commands.

Grades 3–7

- Once students have finished their maze, they can try another team's maze.

Grades 8–12

- Let teams create their own mazes. Once they've finished their maze, they can try another team's maze.

Keep in Mind: This activity may be students' first programming experience. Young people are often users of technology but rarely its controllers or creators. This is a great opportunity to introduce students to computer science and help them practice the important skill of communicating sequential information to help a person execute a task.

Cup Stacking Challenge

In this activity, students will work in teams of 4–5 to stack a set of cups as quickly as possible. This open-ended activity requires students to communicate cooperatively and work together as a team to stack and unstack their cups—without touching them. Teams can try to stack the cups multiple times, improving their communication and techniques with each round.

Time: 5 minutes per round, for as many rounds as you'd like

Materials (per team): plastic cups, 3-foot lengths of string or yarn (1 per student), rubber band (#33), blindfolds (grades 8–12)

Instructions: Introduce the activity. For younger students, you may want to tie their strings to the rubber band before starting. Touching only the strings tied to their team's rubber band and never touching the cups with their hands, students need to use the rubber bands to unstack their stacks of cups and then restack them. (See figure 3.1.) Emphasize that teams need to talk through what they need to do to be successful. Good communication will make or break their success.

Make It Real

Grades PreK–2

- Give teams 5 stacked cups. If teams are successful at stacking and unstacking cups in a single stack, have them try to stack cups in a small pyramid.

Grades 3–7

- Give teams 7 stacked cups. Teams should work together to restack the cups in a pyramid. If they succeed, have them unstack the pyramid and put the cups back into a single stack.

Grades 8–12

- Give teams 12 stacked cups. Teams should work together to restack the cups in a pyramid or whatever tall shape they can create. If they succeed, have them unstack the pyramid and put the cups back into the single stack.

- Have teams pick three people to be the string holders. The remaining team members will be the coaches. Coaches blindfold the string holders and verbally coach them through stacking the cups.

Keep in Mind: While each student is in control of their string, the strings are all connected to the same rubber band. Teams must figure out how much or how little they should pull on the rubber band and which way to move to move their cups around. One person pulling too much will impact everyone else. Teams may want to designate one person as the coach or let everyone talk. What communication strategy works best for each team will vary.

figure 3.1: cup stacking

Draw This

In this activity, students will work in pairs to replicate a picture. One student looks at a sample drawing and communicates what the other student should draw. The student drawing is the Artist, and the student giving directions is the Speaker. The Artist and the Speaker should sit back-to-back so they cannot see each other's papers.

Time: 20–30 minutes

Materials (per pair): pencil, clipboard, blank paper, sample drawings (A, B, or C)

Instructions: Introduce the activity. Have students sit back-to-back, and remind them not to peek at each other's papers. Give the student who is going to be the Speaker a sample drawing. Remind them not to show the Artist. The Speaker describes the drawing to the Artist, and the Artist draws what the Speaker describes. Give partners 5–10 minutes to draw, then have them reveal their work. Allow time for the pairs to discuss what matches and what doesn't. Encourage them to discuss what communication was helpful and what could be improved. Have students switch roles and try with a different drawing.

Make It Real

Grades PK–2	Grades 3–7	Grades 8–12
• Use Sample Drawing A.	• Use Sample Drawing B.	• Use Sample Drawing C.

More for You:

Sample Drawing A, page 86

Sample Drawing B, page 87

Sample Drawing C, page 88

Keep in Mind: This activity is less about a student's ability to draw well and more about being a strong communicator. Encourage students to consider if the Speakers' directions were too hard to follow or were not specific enough. Have students consider what traits a good listener possesses that can help with communication. Remind them that being a good communicator is equal parts listening and speaking.

Skill 4: Collaboration

Collaboration in STEAM goes beyond simply working together. It is being able to recognize the unique strengths and skills each person brings, use those skills to solve a task or problem, and learn from each other. These abilities are often more important than just working side by side.

The Role of the Teacher

The strategies in this section will help foster a collaborative culture in your classroom. Be sure to create teams in various ways. Try pairing students with peers they rarely interact with as well as those they would self-select. Mix up large and small groups, or consider assigning roles to help students explore their strengths or try new things. Celebrate and acknowledge the strengths of each student by bringing them to the attention of the collaborative group.

Collaboration as a STEAM Skill

The ability to collaborate is a skill necessary in all aspects of life. From working together with peers in the classroom to collaborating with colleagues on the job, teamwork often leads to success. Being a skilled collaborator goes beyond working well with others, though. It includes being able to share your expertise to work toward a common goal. The strategies in this chapter encourage students to not only work together but also recognize and tap the talents and strengths of teammates to succeed. Here are some more ideas for building a collaborative classroom.

Give time to reflect. Invite students to write or talk about how and why their group did well (or not so well) in an activity.

Change it up. Let students pick their partners or groups from time to time. Group students in pairs, small groups, or as a full class for the different activities (you might even try a strategy again with different-sized groups). Pay attention to how self-selected groups change over the year and what sorts of skills are being sought after. Always be aware of kids who struggle to find a group. Ask trusted students to invite them, or help them find a group in a subtle way.

Assign roles. Roles like materials manager, timekeeper, communicator, or note-taker can help students understand how they fit into the group dynamic. Assigning roles helps students know what they are supposed to be doing and ensures that one or two students don't take over.

The Strategies

Prepare for Takeoff

You'll need a large space for this strategy! In this activity, students will work in pairs to create and use file folder airplane launchers. Students first test how far their paper airplanes fly when thrown by hand. Then they test how far the planes fly when they use their launchers. Pairs will need to collaborate to improve their airplane's performance with each launch.

Time: 20–40 minutes

Materials (per pair): file folder, printer or origami paper, medium rubber band, ruler, pencil, scissors, stapler, paper clips

Instructions: Introduce the activity and remind students that they should be working together through it. If they have trouble, help them assign roles or come up with ideas for how to collaborate. Each pair will do the following: Mark a 5-x-7-inch rectangle on the file folder, with the folder crease as one long edge of the rectangle. Then cut out the rectangle, making sure to cut through both layers of the folder. Do not cut along the crease; the rectangle should still open like a small folder. With the crease as the bottom, fold down the top edges of the rectangle to meet the crease. Then fold the edges (now at the bottom) up to create a flap large enough to grab on each side. Open the rectangle, and staple the rubber band near one top corner (see figure 4.1).

Once they've built their launcher, have each pair make a paper airplane and practice throwing it to see how far it flies. Then have them try it with the launcher. Close the launcher and stretch the rubber band back and around the end of the folder so it squeezes the folder closed (figure 4.2). Have the pair put their plane in the top of the folder facing the open end, aim the folder, pull out on the flaps to launch their plane (figure 4.3), and track how far it flies. Encourage students to work together to adjust their launchers.

Make It Real

Grades PK–2

- Consider making paper airplanes for students ahead of time.

Grades 3–7

- Have students add paper clips to their planes to change the weight (added weight works best toward the front of the plane).

Grades 8–12

- Give pairs two file folders and have them create two different-sized launchers to test which size makes a better launcher.

More for You: Paper Airplane Folding Instructions, page 89

Keep in Mind: Though the airplanes are made of paper, they can still be dangerous. Remind students never to launch an airplane at anyone, especially at the face. Students who are helping mark where the airplanes landed for their partners should wait until after the airplanes have landed to measure how far they flew.

figure 4.1: launcher flaps

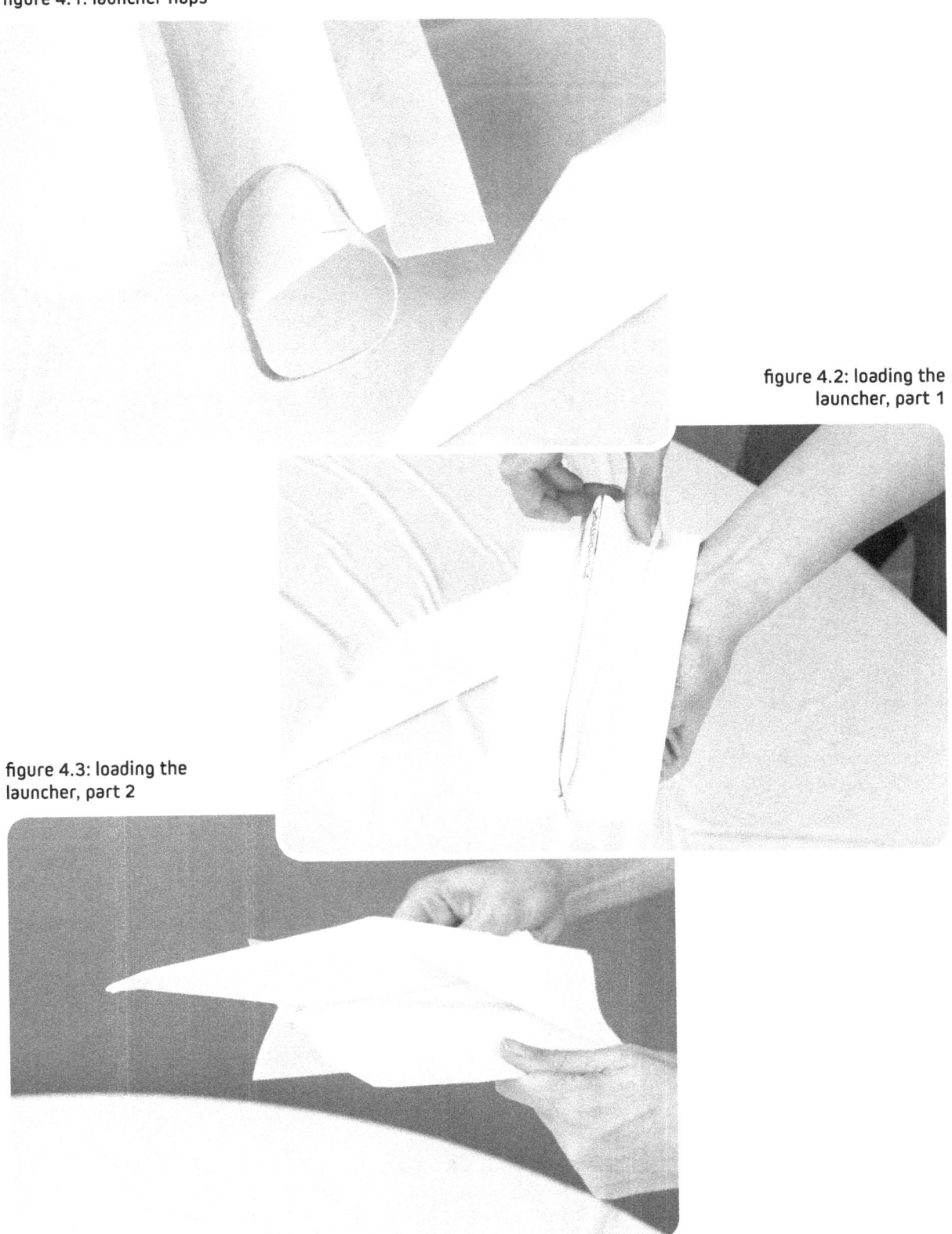

figure 4.2: loading the
launcher, part 1

figure 4.3: loading the
launcher, part 2

Solar S'mores

In this activity, students will work in teams of 3–4 to create solar ovens that harness the energy of the sun to cook s'mores treats. Teams will need to work collaboratively to complete the construction of their ovens.

Time: 40–60 minutes for building, plus cook time

Materials (per team): pizza box (ask for donations), ruler, black marker, scissors, aluminum foil, hot glue (adult use only), plastic wrap, black paper, s'mores supplies (graham crackers, marshmallows, chocolate squares), kabob stick

Instructions: Introduce the activity and explain that each student should make at least one part of their team's solar oven. Each team will do the following: Draw a large square on the top of their team's pizza box and cut along three of the four sides to create a flap with a hinge. Pull up the flap and wrap the bottom side in foil. (Teachers can help hot glue the foil to the box, if needed.) Open the pizza box and line the bottom with black paper. Next, they cut plastic wrap to fit the underside of the pizza box lid, and teachers use hot glue to secure it around the edges of the lid.

Take the boxes to a sunny area, preferably outdoors. Have students assemble their s'mores and set them in the bottom of their team's box. Close the ovens, and use kabob sticks to prop open the foil flaps. In 50–60 minutes, students will have gooey s'mores treats.

Make It Real

Grades PK–2

- Prep materials for students, especially cutting the tops of the pizza boxes.

Grades 3–7

- Consider providing different colors of paper to line the bottoms of the boxes. Have teams consider what they know about colors and heat absorption and reflection when selecting their color.

Grades 8–12

- To increase the difficulty of this activity, consider giving each group the same materials but letting them create solar ovens using their own designs.

More for You: This activity is an introduction to heat as a form of energy while also examining materials science. The aluminum foil is used to reflect the sunlight into the box toward the s'mores while the black paper absorbs the sunlight, increasing the temperature in the oven. The plastic wrap helps trap the heat inside, mimicking an oven door.

Keep in Mind: Whether the solar oven melts the s'mores isn't important. Students can eat their treats either way. This activity is about building trust within a team and working together. Each member of the team must contribute to building the solar oven.

Clean It Up

In this activity, students will work in teams of 3–4 to clean up an oil spill. Explain that an oil spill is when oil is released into a natural area from human activity. Oil spills are dangerous and often deadly to plants and wildlife. Tell students about the 2010 *Deepwater Horizon* disaster, where an oil rig exploded, causing the largest oil spill in history.

Time: 20–60 minutes

Materials (per team): vegetable oil, cocoa powder, plastic shoebox-size container filled halfway with water, cotton balls, plastic spoon, sponge, paper towels, paper plate, plastic cup, cardboard, laptops (grades 8–12)

Instructions: Introduce the activity. Have each team mix 1 teaspoon of cocoa powder into ¼ cup of vegetable oil to create the oil for their oil spill. The team then pours their vegetable oil mixture into their water and tackles cleaning up the spill together. Give students about 5–10 minutes to work, then check on their progress. Discuss what's working and what's not working. How are members of the teams working together to clean up the spills?

Make It Real

- Instead of doing the oil spill activity, prepare trays of different materials for students to explore absorption. Include paper towels, cotton balls, a sponge, foil, and wax paper. Give each group the tray and a small dish of water. Have students test each object in the water to see which absorbs the most.

Grades 3–7

- Challenge teams to stop the oil spill before it reaches the edges of their containers.

Grades 8–12

- Have teams research what strategies were taken to help clean up the 2010 *Deepwater Horizon* spill and what efforts are still being taken to restore the areas affected by the spill.

More for You: Many students will not have heard of the 2010 *Deepwater Horizon* disaster or even the term *oil spill*. Before beginning this activity, spend some time talking about the *Deepwater Horizon* disaster and consider sharing some photos of before and after cleanup efforts, depending on the grade level.

Keep in Mind: To successfully control and clean up their oil spills, students need to work together. They need to communicate which materials are working better than others, where oil is escaping their containment efforts, and how best to tackle the problem.

Water Fountain Challenge

Share with students this fictional problem: the school water fountain is broken and can't be repaired until later in the month. You think you have the right supplies to build some temporary water fountains but need help from students to make enough fountains for the entire school. In this activity, students will work in pairs to build these temporary fountains. I recommend this activity for grades 3 and up since little learners might enjoy playing with the fountains more than completing the challenge.

Time: 45 minutes

Materials (per pair): 2-liter plastic bottle, bendy straw, hot glue (adult use only), duct tape, pitcher of water, bucket, large balloon. **Additional materials for siphon extension:** tall cup, shallow container

Instructions: Prepare materials for students by drilling or cutting a hole the same size as the straw in each plastic bottle, about one-quarter of the way up from the bottom. Introduce the activity. Each pair will do the following: Work together to get the long part of the straw in the hole on the bottle. Students should angle the straw downward and be careful not to pinch it. Once the straw is in, the teacher should put hot glue around the hole to help secure it in place. Once the glue has dried, students put duct tape around the hole to prevent the bottle from cracking and place a bucket under their fountain to catch water. Fill their bottle to the height of the straw.

With the bottle straight, ask students if the water is coming out of the straw. The answer should be no. Have them carefully and only slightly tip their bottles over their buckets. The water should come out of the straws when tipped. Now have students blow up their balloons, pinching them closed to hold the air in, but not tying them. Explain that they will use the balloons like the button on a fountain. Have one student hold the water bucket under the straw while their partner quickly puts the filled-up balloon over the mouth of the bottle. The air will move from the balloon into the bottle and push the water out of the straw. If the water is flowing slowly, the student can push the balloon like the button on the fountain.

Make It Real

- Give students 3–4 additional straws and duct tape. Can students set up a pipe system that reaches farther than a single straw?

- **Siphon Extension (optional):** Have students fill the tall cup with water and place it near the shallow container. Place a straw in the tall cup with the bendy part resting on the lip of the cup and the short part pointing toward the shallow container. Observe what happens. Have students take their straws out of the cups and place one finger over the hole on the short side. Students place the straws back in the cups while keeping a finger on the hole. Have them take their fingers off and observe what happens.

> **More for You:** In the siphon extension, students will also explore air pressure. But this time, they're trapping air in the straws instead of balloons. Once the students release their fingers and the water starts pulling up the straws, it will keep siphoning until all the water is gone from the cup or until the water level in the cup is at the same height as the water level in the other container.

> **Keep in Mind:** Air takes up space even when we can't see it. When the air in the balloon is transferred to the bottle, the water has to move out of the way. Since the straw is there, the water chooses the path of least resistance: up and out of the straw.

Arcade Games

In this activity, students will work in teams of 3–4 to build a working arcade game using recyclable goods. Students need to come up with an original name for their game, rules for playing it, and a difficulty rating. Consider showing images of real arcade games to give students ideas.

Time: multi-day project

Materials: Arcade Game Planning Sheets (1 per team), recyclable materials, packing tape, duct tape, string, art supplies, scissors, box cutter (adult use only), pencils, various sports balls

Instructions: Introduce the activity and show examples of various arcade games. Have each team use the planning sheet to brainstorm and draw an example of the game they want to create before they begin building. They can get as creative as they'd like in the design, materials, and rules for their game. Once they have a plan, it's time to build. You may do one long building session or spread it out over multiple days. Consider asking other school staff to help with the construction phase.

Make It Real

Grades PK–2

- Select what game you want students to create. You might choose a different game for each grade level. Here's an example: bowling game (PK), mini-golf hole (K), knock-down-style carnival game (grade 1), Skee-Ball-style game (grade 2). They can decide the theme and all the other game details.

Grades 3–7

- Consider selecting a few styles of arcade games teams can choose from. They can decide the theme and all the other game details.

Grades 8–12

- Give teams time to research arcade game ideas prior to planning.

More for You: Arcade Game Planning Sheet, page 90

Keep in Mind: Students need to come to a consensus with their teammates on the game they want to create and what its rules and details will be. You may need to step in to help if you notice one or two team members taking over a group.

I'm with the Band

In this activity, each student will create a musical instrument from recyclable materials. Once they have their instruments, help them get into groups of 3–4 to form bands. Using their instruments, students can create their own music or cover a favorite song. You may want to spread this activity over two days: one for instrument building and one for band practice.

Time: 1–2 hours for building and practice

Materials (available for students to choose from): clean recyclable materials; masking tape; scissors; markers; string; rubber bands; balloons; rice, beads, or seeds

Instructions: Introduce the activity. Have students select what type of instrument they want to create. (Students can also invent "new" instruments so long as they can be played in their band.) Give students time to make and test their instruments. Then encourage them to find 2–3 classmates who have different instrument types and form a band.

Students work collaboratively to play their instruments together. Bands can make up their own songs or cover a favorite tune. They do not need to play an entire song, but each member of the band should have a chance to play their instrument.

Make It Real

	Grades 3–7	Grades 8–12
• Provide photographs or real instruments for students to use as models.	• Invite students who play instruments to bring them in and perform for the class.	• Give students time to research examples of instruments made from recyclable materials and look up songs to play.

More for You: Consider sharing a video of the Recycled Orchestra of Cateura as an example of how unconventional materials can be used to create beautiful music.

Keep in Mind: Not all materials make great instruments. Remind students to think creatively about the materials and how they could use them to produce enjoyable sounds together.

Spiraling

In this activity, students will work in teams of 4–5 to move a single marker in a spiral design. All students in the group will be attached to the marker by a piece of yarn or string. One end of the string will be taped to the marker, while a student holds the other end. Communication and collaboration are key to successfully drawing a spiral and completing this activity.

Time: 30 minutes

Materials (per team): 2 markers in different colors, long pieces of yarn or string (1 per student), tape, 2–3 pieces of poster paper

Instructions: Introduce the activity. Each team will do the following: Tape one end of each team member's piece of string to one of the team's markers. Using the other marker, someone on the team draws a large spiral on their poster paper. The team will then work together to trace the spiral as closely as possible, using only the strings to move the marker. (See figure 4.4.) Remind students that the more tension they put on the strings, the straighter their markers will stand.

Make It Real

Grades PK–2

- Prepare materials for students, attaching the strings to the marker before beginning this activity.
- Draw the spiral students will trace.

Grades 3–7

- Challenge teams to try tracing a new spiral in the opposite direction after they've successfully made one tracing.

Grades 8–12

- After teams have made their first tracing, challenge them to draw a spiral without a tracing or write the word *team* using the marker and strings.

Keep in Mind: Each student is controlling their own string and will need to work together with their team to successfully trace the spiral. The amount of work each person is doing will vary depending on where the marker is on the spiral. Teams may decide to designate one person as the leader who helps to guide the team through the design, or they may use another strategy.

figure 4.4: drawing a spiral

Track Plates Challenge

For this activity, you will need a large open area, like a gym, blacktop, or field, for students to test their track plate designs. Students will work in teams of 6–8 to act as the tracks (wheels) on an excavator, using only tape and newspapers to move. Students must work together to build the excavator track and successfully move as a team without damaging it.

Time: 30–45 minutes

Materials (per team): newspaper (you will need a lot), masking tape, scissors

Instructions: Introduce the activity and show students a picture or video of an excavator. Point out how it doesn't have wheels but instead has one large loop of connected track plates. Students will work in teams to build an excavator track and move it together. A team's loop needs to be big enough so all group members can stand up inside it without breaking it.

Once teams have created their tracks, move to a large open area. Teams will stand inside their loops in a single line, with the newspaper track under their feet and over their heads. Now it's time to move! Whoever is in front inside the loop directs the entire team. Teams need to work together to move their track plate loops forward without tearing the paper. Allow students to troubleshoot as they practice making their loops move. They can make repairs or even add additional track plates.

Make It Real

Grades PK–2

- Have students work in teams of 3–4 to create smaller tracks, and use cardboard instead of newspaper so track plates are harder to rip.
- Enlist adult volunteers to help students with the building portion of the activity.

Grades 3–7

- Line teams up at one end of your open area. Once all teams are situated inside their loops, direct them to start moving their track plates forward. This is not a race, but it is important for teams to see which groups are doing a better job of working together.

Grades 8–12

- Once teams get the hang of moving their track plate loops, they can race each other. The team that works together the best will reach the other side first.

Keep in Mind: Students will need a lot of newspaper for this activity. Try to collect old newspapers from the school community, and be sure to recycle materials when you're done.

Three in a Row

This activity is best done in a gym or outside on a blacktop. Three in a Row combines physical activity, teamwork, and problem-solving in a classic tic-tac-toe-style game. Split the class into two teams and assign each team a color. Teams work together to strategize how to both block the other team from getting three in a row while also trying to get three in a row themselves. The first team to get three in a row wins.

Time: 30–45 minutes

Materials: 9 plastic toy hoops, chalk, or masking tape; 2 sets of 9 bean bags in different colors (for example, 9 blue and 9 red)

Instructions: Introduce the activity. Have students help you set up the hoops in a 3 x 3 grid. If you don't have hoops, you can use chalk or masking tape to mark out a grid. Split the class in half, assign each team a color, and give them each a set of nine bean bags in their color. Pass out one bean bag to each student until they are all gone. Explain the rules of the game. Like in tic-tac-toe, teams should try to get three bean bags in a row in the hoops. Each student can use their turn to try to make three in a row or to block the other team from getting three in a row. Unlike tic-tac-toe, teams will be placing their bean bags simultaneously instead of alternating. Have the first person from each team walk to the grid and place their bean bag in a hoop. Once they've placed their bags, students return to their team and the next students in line take a turn placing their bags in any empty hoop. Students cannot go up to the grid until their teammates have returned. Students waiting for their turn should talk with their teams about where to place the next bag. Keep going until a team gets three in a row or all the hoops are filled.

Make It Real

	Grades 3–7	Grades 8–12
• Have students play tic-tac-toe first, alternating turns, before playing the competitive version. Walk students through playing the first round of the game.	• Students can jog or run from their line to the hoops and back. The faster a team moves, the more likely they are to get three in a row first.	• If the game gets too easy, consider setting the hoops up farther away from the teams and using more space in your grid.

Keep in Mind: Though students are not building anything in this activity, they are practicing an important STEAM skill: collaborative problem-solving. Thinking about the solutions and potential barriers simultaneously can help teams develop strategies for getting three in a row. By working together, students can share their strategies for how to win and where they anticipate the other team will try to place their bags.

Spacewalk

This activity is best completed in a large open area where students have room to walk around. Students will work in teams of 5–10, depending on grade level (a larger team increases the difficulty), to complete a story-based team challenge. Explain that they are astronauts in space, and they need to make repairs to their space station. The goal is for the team to get from one side of the space station to the other without falling off into space. They have to be very careful about where they step since there's no gravity in space, and if they make a misstep, they will float away. If a team member has a misstep, they are out of the challenge.

Time: 30–60 minutes

Materials (per team): paper plates (1–2 per student), painter's tape

Instructions: Introduce the activity and mark start and end points for each team. Have teams line up at their start lines, and give each student one or two paper plates. Each team of astronauts will need to complete a spacewalk across their space station, stepping only on parts of the station (paper plates) during their spacewalk. If a student steps anywhere off the plates, they are lost in space and out of the game. Have teams start walking, one student at a time, from the start line to the finish line. Students will need to place plates on the ground to build their paths as they walk. Once teams have mastered their spacewalks, take away a couple of plates for the next round. This will require students to either share the plates or delay a person entering the walk before a teammate is done.

Make It Real

Grades PK–2

- Create students' path for them, placing the plates on the ground in straight or slightly curved lines that they have to walk across like lily pads. If this is too easy, create a dead-end path or a "hazard" (stuffed animal to avoid) to push students to plan their path before starting.

Grades 3–7

- Start by having students walk a set path, then move to having students create a path and pick it up as they travel across the space station.

Grades 8–12

- Students cannot leave any plates behind as they move through their spacewalk. As soon as a plate is empty, it has to be collected. Leaving a plate behind causes space pollution. Teams need to think about how they are going to lay the plates and pick them up while moving their entire team from one end of the space station to the other.

Keep in Mind: This is a problem-solving activity that requires teams to work together to find a solution. Astronauts at space stations are marvelous problem-solvers and collaborators. They cannot call in a repair person or ask for outside help in space. Teams need to work together to figure out how to get from one side of the space station to the other while keeping everyone safe.

Skill 5: Critical Thinking

Critical thinking is the ability to be both a reflective thinker and an independent one. Students who think critically are able to examine a problem and connect ideas to solve it. Critical thinkers are more than just problem-solvers; they are people who can examine different points of view and explore weaknesses and inconsistencies in ideas and arguments. The most important aspect of critical thinking is being able to reflect on your assumptions and decisions so you can continue to grow.

The Role of the Teacher

Consider introducing these critical-thinking activities by showing students an image of a glass frog (*Hyalinobatrachium fleischmanni*) from its translucent stomach side. Ask students to look at the picture and think critically about whether the creature they see is a real type of frog or not. Students need to examine what they already know about frogs and consider the possibility of this frog being real (it is real). It's important as the teacher to never equate critical thinking with how "smart" someone is. Knowing a lot of facts or information does not necessarily make someone a strong critical thinker. The activities in this chapter encourage students to think critically, ask questions, and reflect on their thinking.

The Strategies

Critical Thinking as a STEAM Skill

Critical thinking is a form of emotional intelligence that allows us to think clearly and rationally. This ability to think critically promotes problem-solving both in and out of the classroom. Students who think critically about the world around them are also better able to process information and analyze data. Here are some ideas for fostering critical thinking in your classroom.

Ask rather than answer. When asked to think critically, students may turn to you for the answer. However, having or knowing the answer isn't the point. Instead of giving students the answer, guide them toward understanding through probing questions and encourage them to turn to peers or further research.

Remember that there is no one "right" way. Often there are many ways to solve a problem. Remind students that there is no single right way to complete the activities in this chapter, as long as they stay within the guidelines.

Keep asking. Students often default to what they know and tend to play it safe. Encourage them to get creative and think outside the box. Questions to students about what else they can find, what they could still ask, or what might be missing are all good launching points to encourage critical thinking.

Robotic Hand

When students think of careers related to the human body, they likely default to doctors and nurses, but engineers—especially those working in robotics—must have a deep understanding of the skeletal and muscular systems. In this activity, each student will create a prototype of a robotic hand. Before beginning, spend some time discussing how complex and fascinating the human body is. Share with students that there are 206 bones and 640 muscles in the human body. The hand alone has twenty-seven bones, twenty-seven joints, thirty-four muscles, and over one hundred ligaments and tendons. It is one of the most complex parts of the human body. Ask students to think critically about what knowledge someone might need to create a robotic hand that functions like a human one. Ask them why we might need robotic hands.

Time: 60 minutes; you may choose to spread the activity out over a few days for younger students

Materials (per student): paper, pencil, scissors, 2–3 regular straws, 1 wide straw, kabob stick, clear tape, 5 two-foot pieces of yarn, colored pom poms

Instructions: Introduce the activity. Each student will do the following: Trace their hand on their paper, including the wrist, and cut it out. Then, place their hand back on the hand cutout and mark their knuckles and joints with their pencil. (You may need to model how to do this.) Next, they fold their paper on each mark they made for a joint or knuckle. Then, they cut pieces of straw to match the space between marks and tape the straws between each folded knuckle or joint like bones. They use the kabob stick to thread a piece of yarn through the straws on each finger, leaving the ends out by the wrist and fingertips and tying a knot at each fingertip. (Show students how to tie and tape a large knot at the tip of each finger so the yarn does not pull through.) Then they gather all five pieces of yarn, thread them through the wide straw, and tape the wide straw to the wrist. Tie all five pieces together toward the end of the yarn so they can move each finger individually but also all at once.

Encourage students to practice pulling the pieces of yarn together or individually to try to pick up some of the pom poms. Have a discussion where students think critically about the challenges they experienced when using their robotic hands.

Make It Real

- Precut the straws into ¼-inch and 1-inch pieces for students. Consider creating an example hand, marking the areas where students should place the straws.

- Share a brief history of robotic and prosthetic hands with students, showing examples of how designs have evolved. Have students think critically about the changes to the designs and consider what changes might come in the future.

Grades 8–12

- Have students follow the Robotic Hand Prototype (Grades 8–12) instructions to create a more complex robotic hand.

More for You: Robotic Hand Prototype (Grades 8–12), page 81

Keep in Mind: While students may have seen a robotic hand in the movies or met someone who uses a prosthetic, they may not know that there are many other places and industries where robotic hands are used to perform functions that are dangerous or challenging for a human hand to do. We often see robotic hands used in automotive assembly lines helping with product assembly and more dangerous things like welding.

Tinker Tables

Tinker Tables are designated spaces where students can work independently or collaboratively to reverse-engineer (take apart) broken electronics, and they are a wonderful critical-thinking activity. Most students interact with electronic devices daily but do not understand how they are built or how they work. Providing students with the opportunity to tinker with broken electronics helps pique their natural curiosity to learn about how things work or figure out why something isn't working and repair it.

Time: give students as much or as little time to tinker as you'd like

Materials (for your classroom): safety glasses, pliers, screwdrivers, flashlights, tape measures, hand lenses, bowls or cups (for small pieces), pegboard or toolbox for storage, old or broken electronics and appliances with electrical cords cut off

Instructions: Set up a designated space for tinkering, with tools, materials, and safety equipment. Tell students that all tinkering materials must stay at the Tinker Table. Make sure students know and understand the rules for your Tinker Table, including when they can use the table, how many people can use it at a time, how long they can tinker, and all safety guidelines and procedures (see page 91 for a short list of reminders you might post at the table). Make sure students know what they should recycle, save, and throw out after a tinkering session. As pieces are taken apart and explored, add new items to the Tinker Table. Make sure students know the names of each item and tool and what they are supposed to do or how they should be used. Encourage students to figure out why an item isn't working when they tinker, and explain that taking something apart can help them figure out how to fix the problem. They can try to make repairs if they'd like. Set aside a designated space to store any in-process repairs so that other students don't accidentally take them apart.

Make It Real

Grades PK–2	Grades 3–7	Grades 8–12
• Include simpler items like clocks, calculators, keyboards, and mice for tinkering.	• Include more complex items like computers, video game systems, and appliances for tinkering.	• Challenge students to repair broken items when tinkering.

More for You: Three Rules for Tinkering, page 91

Keep in Mind: Students aren't often given the opportunity to think critically about why something might have stopped working or even how things work. Many electronics and appliances hide their mechanisms internally, so the user never sees them. No matter a student's age, taking apart items they encounter in their everyday lives helps them better understand how things work. Tinkering also helps students of all ages practice fine-motor skills. **Always consider any risk of opening up or taking apart an item before putting it at the Tinker Table.**

Marble Run

Marble runs require the builder to think about all the possible outcomes for the marble moving through the run. Being able to plan ahead and anticipate what might come is critical thinking. In this activity, students will work in groups of 3–4 to create a marble run that moves a marble from one location to another using ramps, tunnels, tubes, and tracks. This physical science activity explores kinetic and potential energy, as well as gravity, speed, friction, and momentum.

Time: multi-day project

Materials (per team): medium or large cardboard box (no deeper than a shoebox), cardboard tubes, paper cups, craft sticks, masking tape, marble, scissors, hot glue and X-Acto knife (adult use only)

Instructions: Introduce the activity and share a model marble run you created (or show a video of one). Explain that each team needs to create a marble run that moves their marble from the top of the box to a cup at the bottom. The marble cannot just drop to the bottom. It needs to roll at least part of the way. Have each team draw the design for their marble run in the box first. They can pick out their materials as they work and secure the pieces of their marble run in the box, following their design. Give groups time to test their designs and make improvements. Invite them to show how their marble run works to the rest of the class.

Make It Real

- Precut cardboard strips and tubes. Use large marbles to avoid choking hazards.

Grades 3–7

- Consider adding in a stopwatch to see how fast the marbles complete each run.

Grades 8–12

- Students can build along classroom walls and furniture over multiple class periods to create a roller-coaster marble run. Their run needs to have one incline, one drop, and one loop, but the rest of the design is up to them.

Keep in Mind: Students will need to tweak their designs to keep the marble moving from the start to the finish of the run. If a team is stuck, prompt them to think critically about the problem. They might need to move part of the run higher or lower. How are gravity, speed, and inertia working to keep their marble moving?

Recycled Cars

The ability to look at an item designed for one purpose and see its potential to be used for other purposes is a critical-thinking skill. In this activity, students will create model cars out of recyclable goods. Consider setting up recycle collection bins in the cafeteria and asking families to help collect materials at home.

Time: 45 minutes; you may want to spread this activity across two days for younger grades

Materials (per student): empty juice box, 4 identical-size bottle caps, 2 toothpicks, painter's tape, bendy straw, large balloon

Instructions: Poke holes in the centers of the bottle caps ahead of time. Introduce the activity. Each student will do the following: Put a bottle cap on each end of their toothpicks so each toothpick has two bottle caps. Attach the toothpick wheels to the bottom of the juice box with painter's tape. Make sure the tape is loose enough for the toothpicks to spin. On the top of their juice box, tape the long part of their straw down the center of the car, leaving some overhang to blow into. They place their balloon on the short end of the straw and tape it in place.

Have students blow in the end of their straws to fill up the balloons. Have them place their fingers over the open end of the straws until they set down their cars on a smooth flat surface (see figure 5.1). Then, they release their fingers and watch the cars move. Allow students to try this a few times. Then encourage them to try their cars on different surfaces, such as carpet and tile, and to think critically about what surface the car drives the best on.

Make It Real

Grades PK–2

- Have students race their cars to see which car travels the farthest.

Grades 3–7

- Have students add weight to their cars with coins, washers, or heavy screws and bolts and see how this changes how cars move.

Grades 8–12

- Students make more complex recyclable cars (see More for You).

More for You: Recycled Cars (Grades 8–12), page 82

Keep in Mind: The more students fill their balloons or stretch their rubber bands (grades 8–12), the farther their cars can travel. Strategically placing weight on their cars helps improve the momentum of the cars and therefore also improves the distance cars can travel. Allow time for students to explore these factors and see if they can get their cars to travel farther.

figure 5.1: juice box car

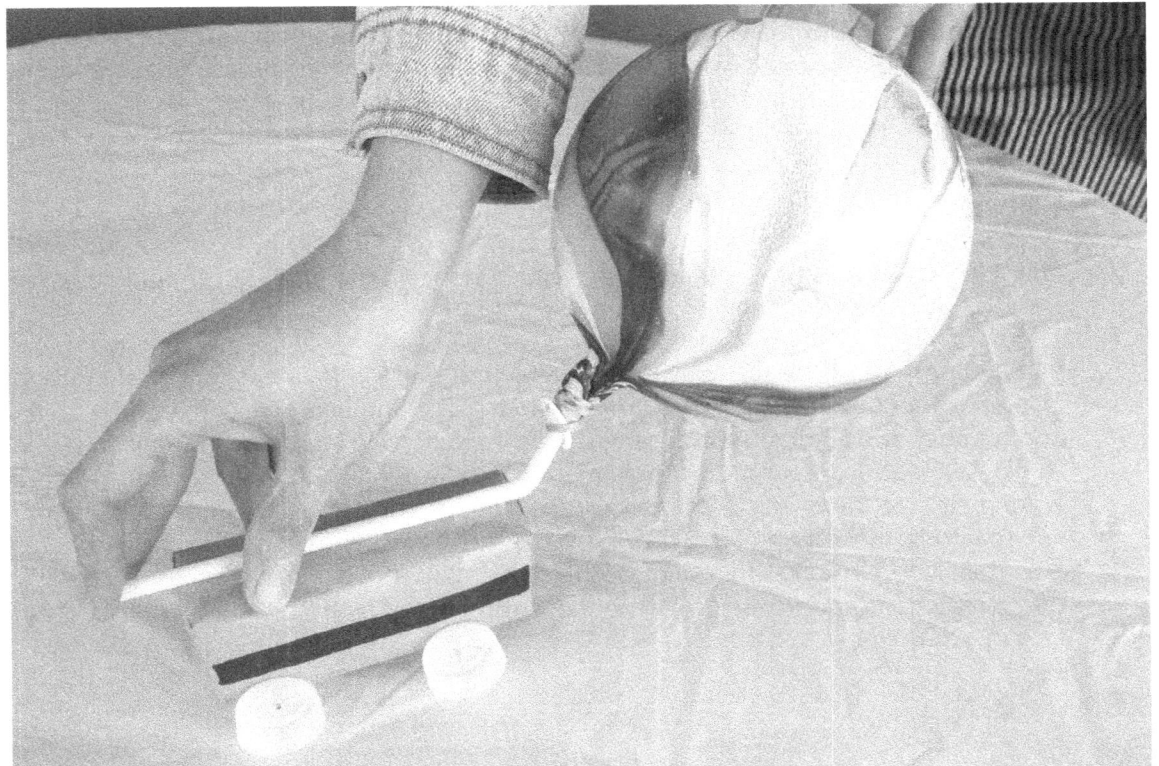

Frog Jump

In this activity, students will individually test and collect data on how long of a jump a frog can make. Younger students will use plastic frogs, while older students will create their own origami frogs. Students will have multiple opportunities to improve their frog jump and will need to think critically about their approach to improve their frogs' performance.

Time: 20–30 minutes

Materials (per student): 1 toy jumping frog (students in grades 8–12 can fold origami frogs instead), painter's tape, ruler

Instructions: Introduce the activity. Tape a 10-foot piece of painter's tape to the ground in an area without any obstacles (you may need to make multiple lines, depending on time and number of students). Pass out the plastic frogs or have students fold their origami frogs. Have each student predict how many jumps it will take to move their frog 10 feet and write their prediction. Students can practice jumping their frogs anywhere but the 10-foot line to inform their predictions. Now have them test their predictions on the line, counting how many jumps it takes for their frogs to move 10 feet. What was the difference between their predictions and the actual number of jumps? How might a student improve their frog's performance?

Make It Real

Grades K-2

- Students can practice subtraction by finding the difference between their predictions and the actual number of jumps.

Grades 3–7

- Have students complete multiple trials of the frog jump to improve their frogs' performance.

Grades 8–12

- Students make an origami frog to test. Challenge them to make adjustments to the frog's design between trials to improve performance.

More for You: Origami Frog Folding Instructions, page 92

Keep in Mind: This activity encourages students to think critically about their predictions. They have to use what minimal knowledge they have about their frogs' jumping ability based on practice jumps to predict what they think their frogs can do. Being able to think critically about the best way to jump their frogs can help improve their frogs' performance.

Cinderella's Cobbler

In this activity, students will work in pairs to design and create a replacement shoe for Cinderella. The glass slippers she has keep falling off her feet and aren't working for her. Students should think critically about Cinderella's needs and design a replacement shoe that meets those needs. Tell students that they do not have to design another glass slipper. They can create any type of shoe, as long as they can justify why it would work for Cinderella.

Time: 20–30 minutes

Materials (for students to choose from): newspapers, paper cups, masking tape, clear packing tape, scissors, string, "Cinderella" story (optional)

Instructions: Introduce the activity and read or share the story of Cinderella. Have students consider the features they do and do not like in a shoe before they begin building their replacement shoes. Give pairs 15–20 minutes to make one shoe each, using the available materials. After students are done making their shoes, have each pair share their shoe design and explain why it would work for Cinderella.

Make It Real

- Students can draw shoe replacements instead of creating them and share with the class.

Grades 3–7

- Encourage students to examine their own shoes for ideas. Remind them to think about what they like and do not like about their shoes and how that could help Cinderella.

Grades 8–12

- Consider having students make their shoes waterproof. They will need to think critically about what materials they have that might protect the newspaper from water. (You may need to add plastic wrap and foil to the selection of materials.)

Keep in Mind: Students do not have to create a high-heeled replacement for Cinderella, but they can if they wish. If they think a sneaker or sandal is a better choice, they can create one, but they will need to justify their decision.

50 Strategies for Teaching STEAM Skills—136021

Paper Chains

This activity can be done in pairs, in groups, or individually. Students will work to create the longest paper chain possible using only one sheet of paper. Students will need to think critically about how best to use the limited materials to create their chain.

Time: 20–30 minutes

Materials (per student, pair, or group): one sheet of paper, scissors, clear tape, tape measure

Instructions: Introduce the activity and show younger students images of both a metal chain and a paper chain to give them some context for the challenge. Tell students that once they cut the paper, they cannot undo that cut, but they can tape things back together again. Give students 5–10 minutes to make their first chains, then measure them. Talk about what worked well and not so well for making the longest chain. Give students new pieces of paper and challenge them to make another chain that is longer than their first ones. Give them 5–10 minutes to work, and then measure the chains. Display the paper chains created by the class.

Make It Real

Grades PK–2

- Talk about what students did to make their second chains longer than their first.

Grades 3–7

- Challenge students to make a third paper chain that is longer than their first two. Have them find the average length of their three paper chains.

Grades 8–12

- Have students make three chains and graph the lengths on a piece of chart paper. The student, pair, or group with the longest chain explains what strategy they used.

Keep in Mind: Students will approach this challenge in a variety of ways, some better than others. All students are given chances to improve their design during this challenge. However, taping paper strips together without making it a chain does not count.

Help the Hiker

One of the major risks of hiking is getting hurt on the trail in an area not easily accessed. In those instances, rescue workers must use unconventional tools to get hikers off the trail and to safety. In this activity, students will work in teams of 3–4 to build a device to help rescue an injured hiker. They need to think critically about how they can keep their hiker safe and secure while transporting them using the designated transport method.

Time: 30–60 minutes

Materials (per team): paper cup, straws, paper towel tubes, craft sticks, cardboard, masking tape, paper clips, string, scissors, large bolts, paper doll; **additional materials for grades 8–12:** wooden spools, wooden craft wheels

Instructions: Introduce the activity. Whatever rescue device each team makes, they must include a rescue basket that fits the hiker (paper doll) lying down and the bolts that represent the weight of the hiker (see below). The hiker needs to be secured in the basket so that they do not fall off when being moved. Give teams time to work on making their rescue devices. Encourage them to test and improve their designs as they work. After they finish, allow time for teams to demonstrate how their rescue devices work. Have them explain how they will rescue the hiker.

Make It Real

- Students create a rescue basket that can be carried by rescue workers. The rescue basket should be able to hold the paper hiker as well as 5 bolts, representing the weight of the hiker.

Grades 3–7

- Students create a rescue basket that is picked up by a helicopter to fly a hiker out. They must include a piece of string that can be pulled up to the helicopter. The rescue basket should be able to hold the paper hiker as well as 8 bolts, representing the weight of the hiker.

Grades 8–12

- Students create a rescue basket and pulley system that can pull a hiker out of a canyon. The pulley system should be attached to the edge of a desk and should pull the basket from the floor up to the edge of the desk. The rescue basket should be able to hold the paper hiker as well as 8 bolts, representing the weight of the hiker.

More for You: Paper Hiker Template, page 93

Keep in Mind: It is equally important to secure the hiker in the basket as it is to fit them in it. Dropping a hiker while trying to move them to safety could result in additional injuries. Remind students to think about how they might secure the hikers to the baskets. Encourage them to think critically about how they would want to be secured and transported if they were the injured hiker.

Circle Spinners

In this activity, each student will create an old-fashioned spinning toy using geometry, physics, and art. Students will need to think critically about their geometric art and how their design transforms when in motion.

Time: 30 minutes

Materials (per student): paper plate, cup (grades PK–2) or compass (grades 3–7), pencil, ruler, scissors, markers, penny; **additional materials for string spinner extension:** cardboard, glue, paper, 16-inch piece of string, thumbtack

Instructions: Introduce the activity and remind students that their pennies should not go in their mouths. Each student will do the following: Draw a circle by tracing a paper cup or using a compass on their paper plate. Use a ruler to divide their circle into fourths or sixths. Then color the circle, creating a new geometric design in each section, and cut it out. Cut a slit that is slightly smaller than the penny in the center of the circle. Push their penny into the slit. (See figure 5.2.) Holding the penny between their fingers, spin their spinner on a hard surface. It may take a few tries to get the spinner to spin. As their spinners spin, invite students to view them and think critically about how the designs they created look when spun.

String Spinner Extension: Each student will do the following: Create and cut out two circles from paper. Then create a third circle on a piece of cardboard and cut it out. Glue one paper circle to each side of the cardboard circle and decorate each side with a geometric design. Using a thumbtack, punch two holes through the center of the circle and thread one end of a string through each hole to create a loop. (See figure 5.3.) Tie the two ends together. Wind up the spinner by holding the string loops in each hand, and watch their designs spin. Students will need to think critically about how to get their circles to spin and keep on spinning.

Make It Real

Grades PK–2

- Model how to draw different types of lines (zigzag, squiggle, diagonal, etc.). Encourage students to think critically about how they could use different lines and shapes in their designs.

Grades 3–7

- If time permits, invite students to add to their geometric designs to change how their spinners look when spun.

Grades 8–12

- Students create string spinners following the String Spinner Extension instructions.

Keep in Mind: Some students may not be able to spin the penny or string spinner on the first try. Both of these spinning activities will require students to use trial and error to get their circles to spin. If students become frustrated, ask them to think about what isn't working and what changes they could make. Problem-solving is a critical-thinking skill that students need time to practice, especially when frustrated.

figure 5.2: penny spinner

figure 5.3: string spinner

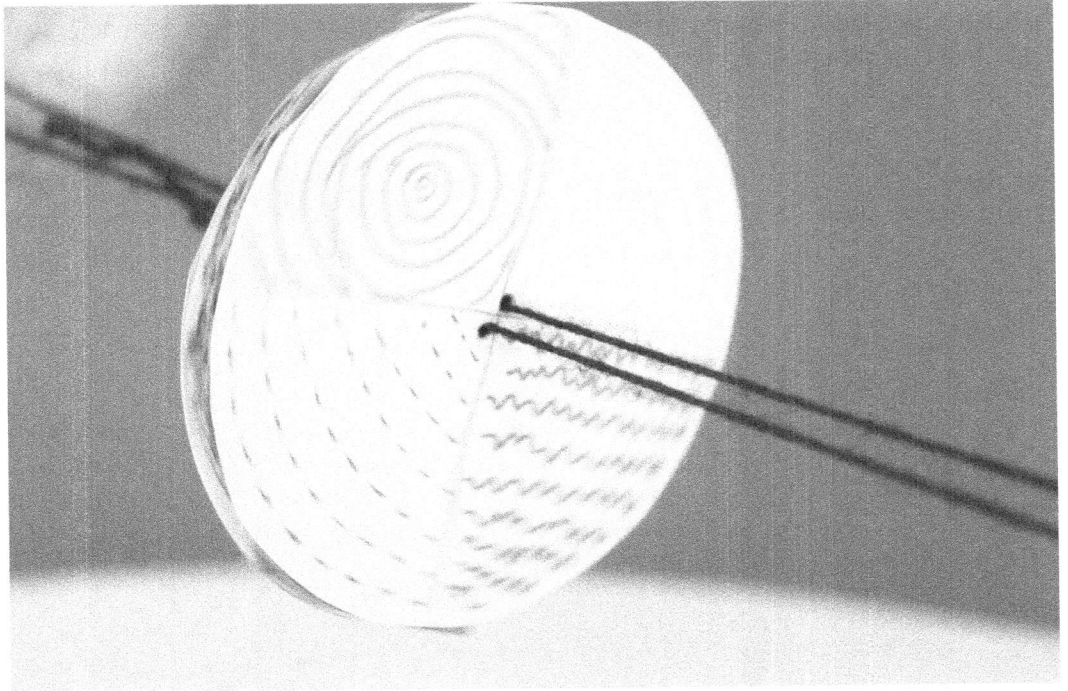

Domino Drop

In this activity, students will explore cause and effect using dominoes in a domino drop challenge. They will also need to use their critical-thinking skills to design and improve their domino drops. Students will work in teams of 3–4 to set up dominoes to create a domino chain reaction. These can be as simple or as complicated as students can imagine and create. Encourage students to use blocks, books, and other objects to increase the complexity of their domino drops.

Time: 20–30 minutes

Materials (per team): dominoes (multiple sets), wooden blocks, books or other classroom objects

Instructions: Introduce the activity and show a video of a domino drop. Talk about cause and effect. Have teams set up simple domino drops and test their chain reactions. If a team's drop gets stuck at any point, they need to think critically about what to change so all the dominoes fall. Once a team has created a successful simple chain reaction, invite them to make a new one, trying more complex shapes and designs and even incorporating classroom furniture and materials.

Make It Real

Grades PK–2

- Give students larger dominoes to build their domino drops. You can also use hardcover books. Have students start with 10 dominoes or books. Once they build a successful chain reaction, they can add more pieces to their chains.

Grades 3–7

- Give groups 20 dominoes to start. Once each group creates a simple chain reaction with the 20 dominoes, they can add more. Encourage groups to try making spirals or having the dominoes go up and over blocks or other items.

Grades 8–12

- Challenge students to create complex designs and think critically about how a chain reaction might work in a multi-tiered domino drop.

Keep in Mind: There are hundreds of ways to design domino chain reactions. Challenge students to be as creative as possible. Remind them that setting up the dominoes is just as important as knocking them down. Students will need a stable surface to work on that isn't easily shaken or shifted. Students need to think critically about their designs and the cause-and-effect relationship of each domino on the next one. This challenge requires students to test and improve their designs.

Bibliography

These resources were referenced in the writing of this book.

Brown, Bryan. 2019. *Science in the City: Culturally Relevant STEM Education*. Cambridge, MA: Harvard Education Press.

Froschauer, Linda (ed.). 2016. *Bringing STEM to the Elementary Classroom*. Arlington, VA: NSTA Press.

Heroman, Cate. 2017. *Making and Tinkering with STEM: Solving Design Challenges with Young Children*. Washington, DC: NAEYC.

Honey, Margaret, and David E. Kanter (eds.). 2013. *Design, Make, Play: Growing the Next Generation of STEM Innovators*. New York: Routledge.

Jolly, Anne. 2017. *STEM by Design: Strategies and Activities for Grades 4–8*. New York: Routledge.

Larmer, John, John Mergendoller, and Suzy Boss. 2015. *Setting the Standard for Project-Based Learning*. Arlington, VA: ASCD.

Martinez, Sylvia, and Gary Stager. 2019. *Invent to Learn: Making, Tinkering, and Engineering in the Classroom*. Torrance, CA: Constructing Modern Knowledge Press.

Sousa, David, and Thomas Pilecki. 2018. *From STEM to STEAM: Brain-Compatible Strategies and Lessons That Integrate the Arts*. Thousand Oaks, CA: Corwin.

Windschitl, Mark, Jessica Thompson, and Melissa Braaten. 2018. *Ambitious Science Teaching*. Cambridge, MA: Harvard Education Press.

Tessellations (Grades 8–12)

figure 6.1: making the template

figure 6.2: tessellation

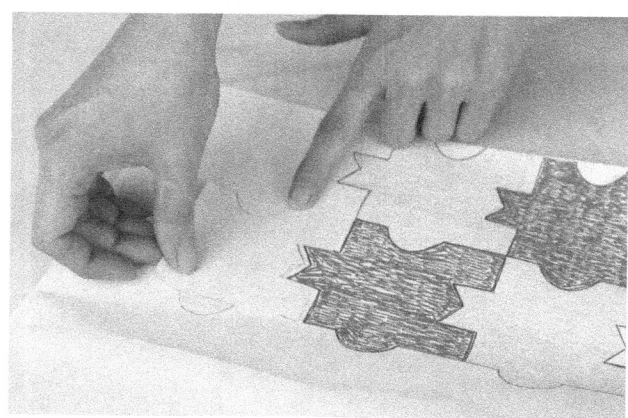

Materials (per student): square sticky note, pencil, tape, scissors, blank paper

Instructions:

1. Draw a shape on one edge of the sticky note.
2. Cut out the shape and slide it across the sticky note, taping it to the opposite side.
3. Draw a shape on one of the remaining straight sides.
4. Cut out this shape and slide it across the sticky note, taping it to the opposite side.
5. Use this new shape for the tessellation.

Zoetropes

figure 6.3: zoetrope

Materials (per student): dark-colored paper, pencil, ruler, scissors, tape, paper plate, white paper

Instructions: Consider showing an example of a zoetrope you created. Explain that *zoetrope* means "wheel of life," coming from the Greek words *zoe* (meaning "life") and *tropos* (meaning "turning"). Zoetropes were designed as Victorian animation toys. The spinning drum (in this case, the plate) creates the illusion of motion using a sequence of still pictures.

1. Cut the dark paper into a long rectangle that can be made into a cylinder that fits inside the paper plate. Lay the rectangle flat and use the ruler to make a mark every inch on a long side. At the marks, cut a slit 1 inch deep and $\frac{1}{8}$ inch wide. Once the slits are cut, the dark paper should look like a fence. Tape the ends together to form a cylinder with the fence at the top.

2. Tape the cylinder in place on the plate.

3. Use the pencil to poke a hole in the center of the plate, in the middle of the cylinder. Put the pencil through and tape it into place as a handle.

4. Cut out a strip of white paper that is long enough to fit as a smaller cylinder inside of the dark cylinder. The white cylinder should be shorter than the notches cut in the dark paper. On the white paper, create a mini story for one character—a simple sequence that shows a single character doing an action, changing slightly from image to image.

5. Once the drawings are done, tape the white paper into a cylinder, with the drawings facing out, and attach it to the plate inside of the dark cylinder to finish the zoetrope.

6. Spin the plate on the pencil and practice looking at the image inside at different angles. Practice spinning the zoetrope at different speeds.

Cloud in a Jar (Grades 8–12)

Materials: glass jars with lids (1 per student; do not use plastic), 1-cup measuring cups, boiling water, food coloring, ice cubes, aerosol hairspray

Instructions: Introduce the activity. Set out the materials for the students to measure out as needed at each table.

1. Pour 1 cup of boiling water into a glass jar. Add food coloring to the water. This will help identify where the water and the cloud are.

2. Spray the hairspray onto the boiling water in the jar and immediately put on the lid. Then place 3–5 ice cubes on top of the jar. Observe what happens.

3. After the cloud forms in the jar, open the jar and let the cloud out. Watch as the cloud moves out of the jar.

Have students give a weather report about what they saw. They can give their weather reports to partners or the whole class, or you can set up a laptop and allow them to record themselves.

Robotic Hand Prototype (Grades 8–12)

figure 6.4: robotic hand

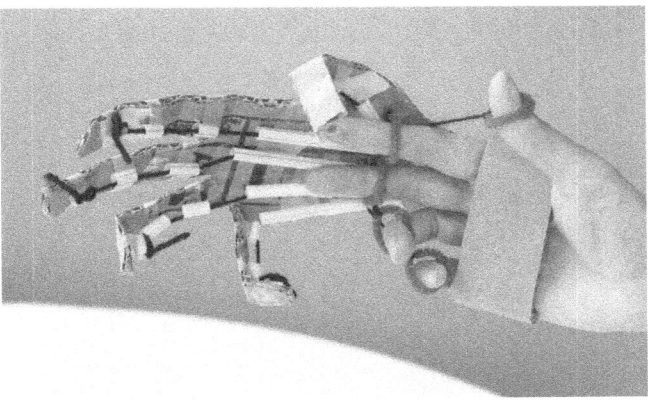

Materials (per student): piece of cardboard large enough for the student's hand, pencil, scissors, 2–3 straws, clear tape, kabob stick, 5 one-foot pieces of yarn, pipe cleaner, colored pcm poms

Instructions:

1. Trace a hand, including the wrist, on the piece of cardboard, and cut it out. Then cut out a rectangular piece that fits around the cardboard hand like a cuff.

2. Place a hand back on the cutout hand and mark the knuckles and joints with a pencil. (You may want to model how to do this.) Then fold the cardboard at each joint or knuckle.

3. Cut 18 pieces of straw to be the bones of the robotic hand, and tape them between the joints. Bones need to be short enough that the joints can bend. Then, tape five pieces of straw on the palm toward the wrist, modeling the bones in a human hand. Leave room for a cardboard wrist cuff.

4. Use the kabob stick to thread the five pieces of yarn through the straws on each finger. Leave an end of each piece out by the wrist and fingertips. Tie a knot at the tip of each finger and tape it down so that the yarn doesn't pull out of the straws.

5. Cut the pipe cleaner into small pieces that can be wrapped around the tips of the operator's fingers. Thread the yarn from the straws through the palm straws and tie each end to a different pipe cleaner ring.

6. Attach the cuff to the bottom of the robotic hand's wrist. Hold on to this cuff when operating the prosthetic hand.

7. Operate the robotic hand using the pipe cleaner rings attached to the pieces of yarn. Each finger should be able to move individually and also all at once. Practice pulling the yarn pieces together or individually and try to pick up some of the pom poms on the tray.

Have a discussion where students think critically about the challenges they experienced when using the robotic hand.

Recycled Cars (Grades 8–12)

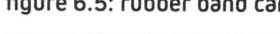

figure 6.5: rubber band car

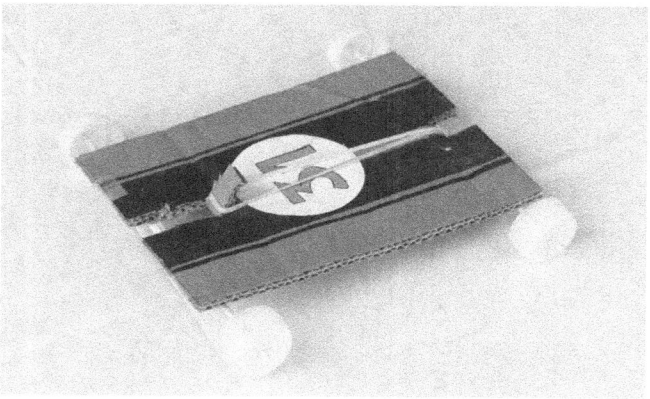

© Maria Zuchora-Walske

Materials (per student): 4 identical-size plastic bottle caps, ruler, cardboard, scissors, 2 straws, hot glue, 2 kabob sticks, large rubber band, heavy screws or bolts

Instructions:

1. Poke a hole in the center of each bottle cap.

2. Cut out a rectangle of cardboard roughly 5 x 7 inches. Write *Front* and *Back* on the narrow ends of the cardboard rectangle.

3. On the Front end, cut two slits about half an inch apart near the center, and fold up the cardboard between the slits.

4. Cut two half-inch pieces of straw, and hot glue one piece to each corner on the Back end of the rectangle, with the holes of the straw facing each other. Cut out a small notch between these two straws, and slide a skewer through both pieces of straw.

5. Put one bottle cap on the end of the skewer and secure it with tape or hot glue. Then cut the other side of the skewer down, leaving only enough to mount the second wheel on the end.

6. Hot glue a piece of straw running across the Front end of the cardboard. Put the second skewer through and mount the wheels.

7. On the Back end of the car, tie the rubber band in the center of the skewer. Then stretch it from the back skewer to the front cardboard tab and loop it around.

8 Pull back on the car to wrap the rubber band around the back skewer, then let go and watch the car move.

9. Think critically about how heavy screws or bolts could be attached to the car design to change how well it runs. Add weight and test it out.

Origami Crane Folding Instructions

1.

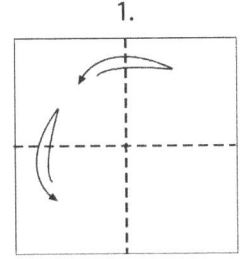

Fold vertically and unfold. Then fold horizontally and unfold.

2.

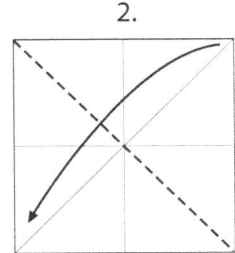

Fold diagonally.

3.

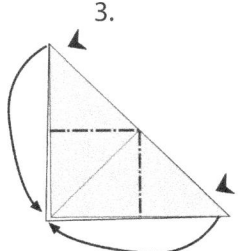

Bring one point along folded edge to the center, opening as you go to form a square. Turn over and repeat on other side.

4.

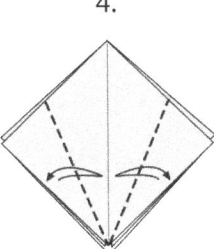

Fold sides of top layer to middle and unfold.

5.

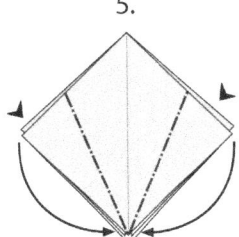

Fold the outside corners in to create a kite shape.

6.

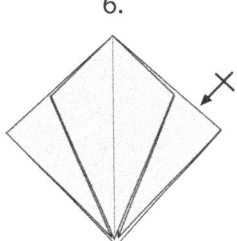

Repeat steps 4 and 5 on the other side.

7.

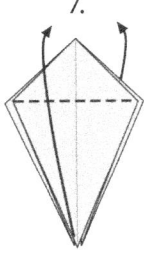

Open your kite shape into a diamond by lifting up the top layer (as if creating a boat) and pressing it down. Flip over paper and repeat on other side.

8.

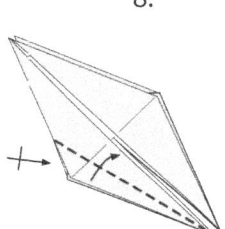

Fold the outside corner in to the middle on both side. Flip over your paper and repeat on other side.

9.

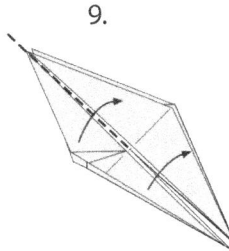

10.

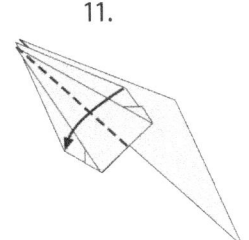

Fold up the bottom point to create your crane's tail.

11.

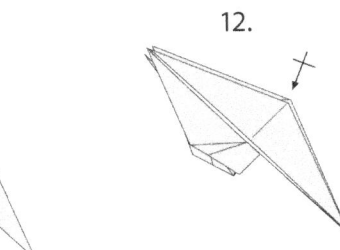

12.

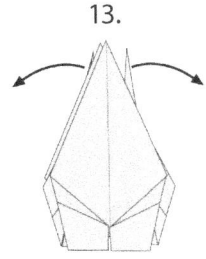

Repeat steps 8–11 on this side to create your crane's neck.

13.

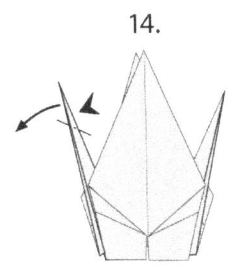

Pull out on your crane's tail and neck.

14.

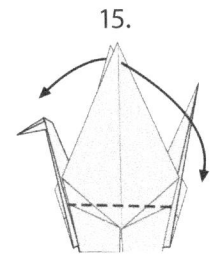

Fold down the tip of the neck to make a head.

15.

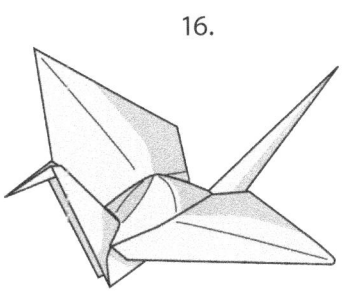

Fold down the wings on each side.

16.

Balancing Act Activity Sheet

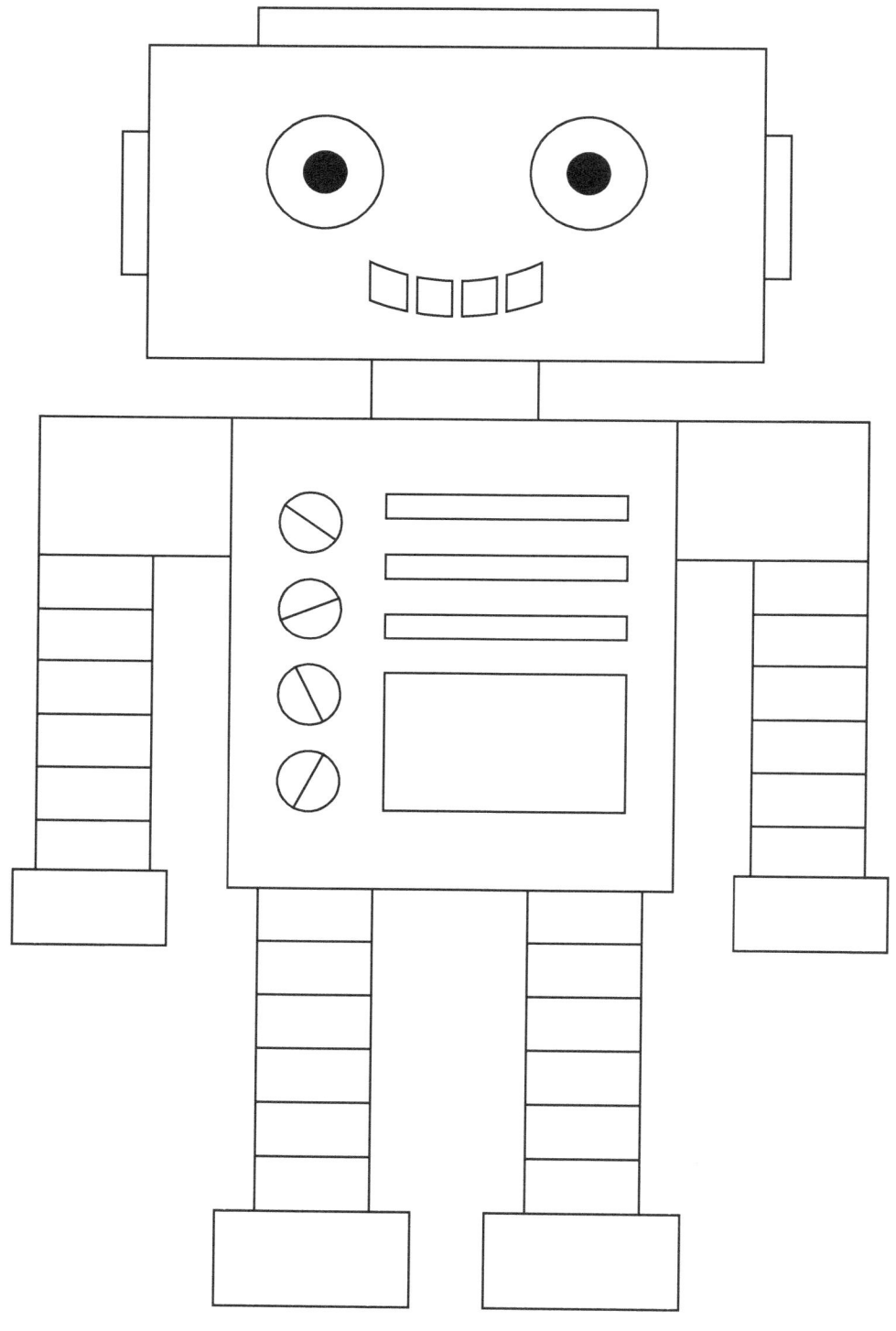

 50 Strategies for Teaching STEAM Skills—136021

Circle Template

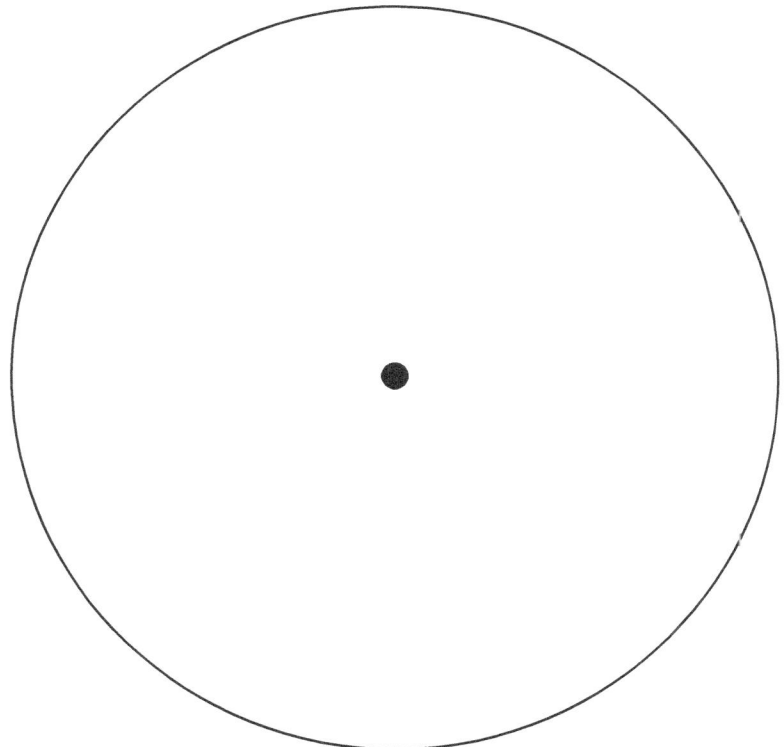

Sample Drawing A

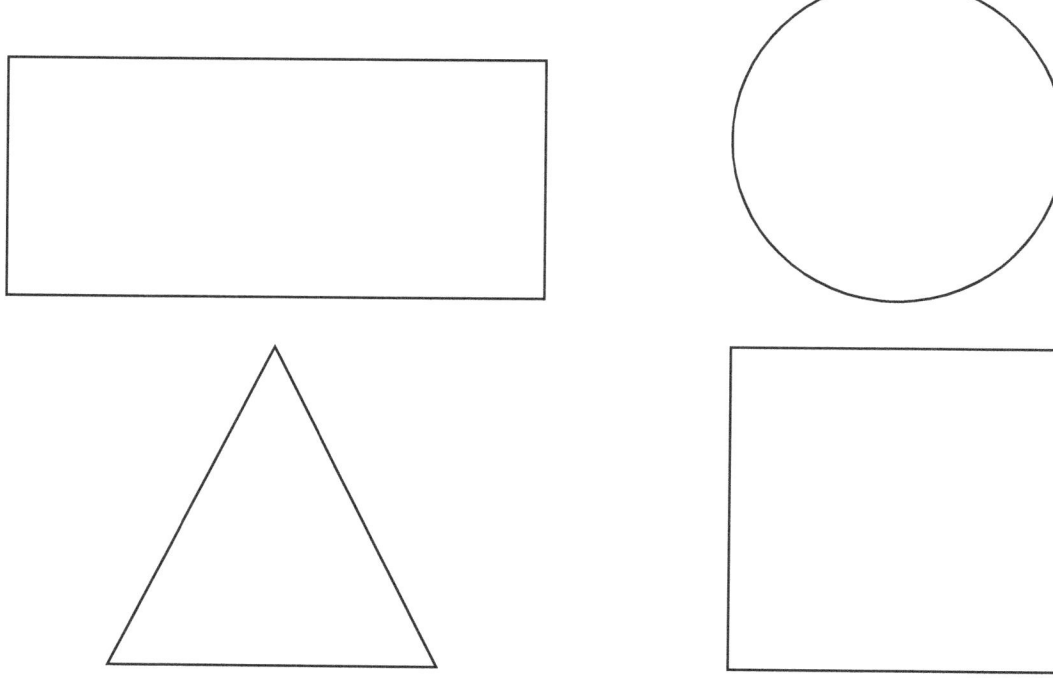

✂ --

50 Strategies for Teaching STEAM Skills—136021

Sample Drawing B

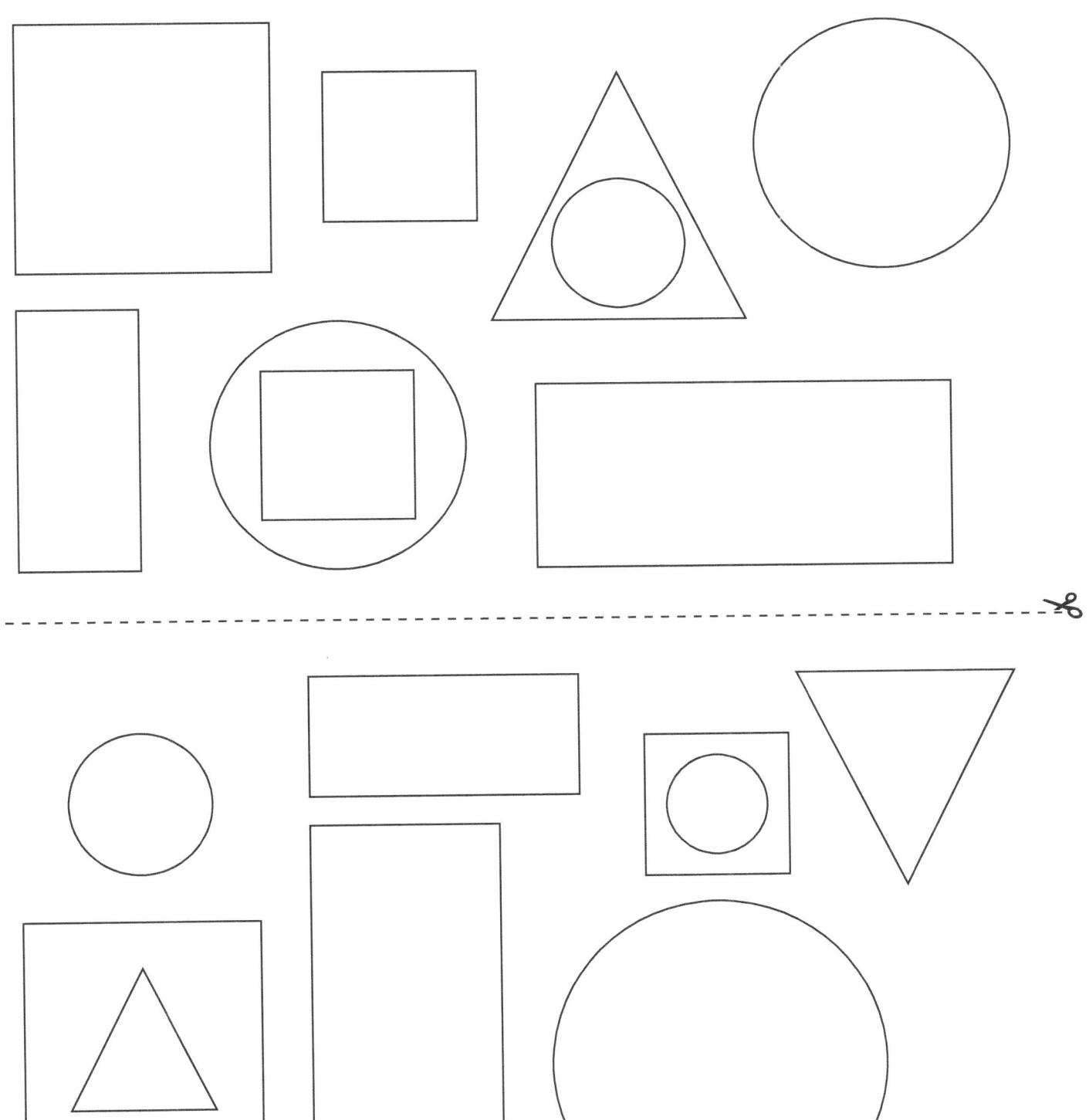

Sample Drawing C

Paper Airplane Folding Instructions

1.

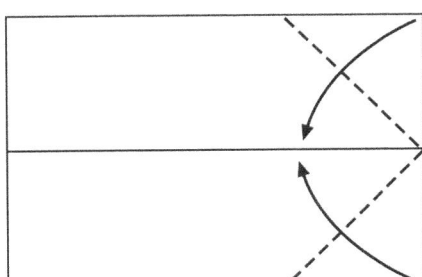

2.

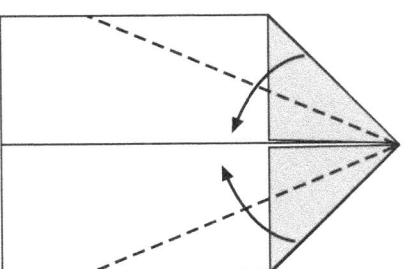

3.

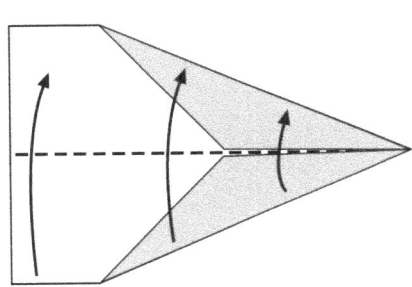

4.

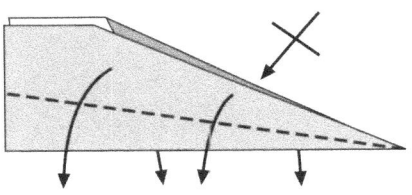

5.

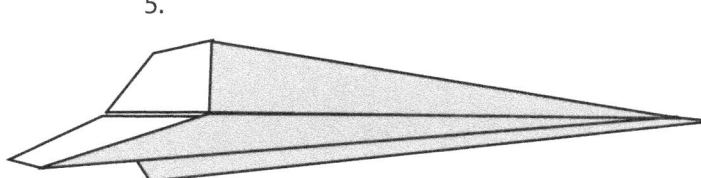

Arcade Game Planning Sheet

Team members: _____

Imagine what your team's arcade game will look like in the space below.

```
┌──────────────────────────────────────────────────────────┐
│                                                            │
│                                                            │
│                                                            │
│                                                            │
│                                                            │
│                                                            │
│                                                            │
│                                                            │
│                                                            │
└──────────────────────────────────────────────────────────┘
```

Now decide on your game's name and at least three rules for playing.

Our game is called: _____

Rule 1: _____

Rule 2: _____

Rule 3: _____

We give this game a _____ star rating for difficulty.

☆ ☆ ☆ ☆ ☆

Three Rules for Tinkering

1. Always wear goggles when tinkering.

2. Use tools in the ways they're intended to be used. All tools must stay at the Tinker Table.

3. Clean up after yourself when you finish tinkering. Save, recycle, or throw away materials. Put away tools and goggles.

Origami Frog Folding Instructions

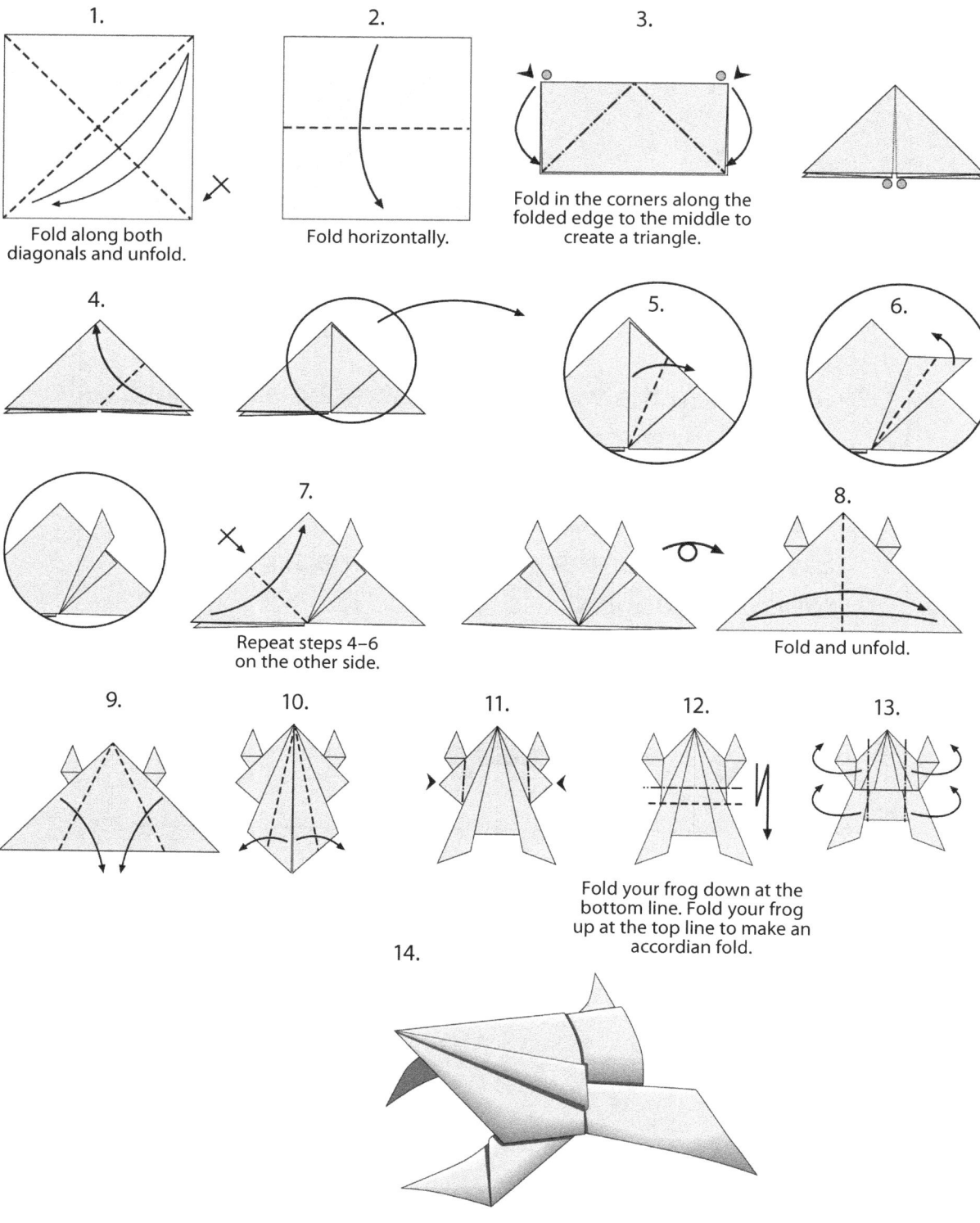

1.
Fold along both
diagonals and unfold.

2.
Fold horizontally.

3.
Fold in the corners along the
folded edge to the middle to
create a triangle.

4.

5.

6.

7.
Repeat steps 4–6
on the other side.

8.
Fold and unfold.

9.

10.

11.

12.
Fold your frog down at the
bottom line. Fold your frog
up at the top line to make an
accordian fold.

13.

14.

Paper Hiker Template

50 Strategies for Teaching STEAM Skills—136021

Additional Print and Online Resources

Books

Ambitious Science Teaching by Mark Windschitl, Jessica Thompson, and Melissa Braaten (Harvard Education Press, 2018). This book shares core practices for science instruction.

Creativity 101 by James C. Kaufman (Springer Publishing Co., 2016). Written by a leading expert on the psychology of creativity, this book shares theories and research on what we know about creativity and how it operates in individuals and society.

Design, Make, Play, edited by Margaret Honey and David E. Kanter (Routledge, 2013). This book shares ways to inspire and motivate students in learning about science and technology.

An Educator's Guide to STEAM by Cassie Quigley and Danielle Herro (Teachers College Press, 2019). This book explains the differences between STEM and STEAM and how you can engage students in STEAM.

From STEM to STEAM, second edition, by David A. Sousa and Tom Pilecki (Corwin, 2018). Classroom strategies, tools for professional development, and planning frameworks for transitioning from STEM to STEAM are explored.

Invent to Learn by Sylvia Libow Martinez and Gary Stager (Constructing Modern Knowledge Press, 2019). This book helps educators bring the maker movement into their classrooms.

Science in the City by Bryan A. Brown (Harvard Education Press, 2019). This book links research on urban science teaching to practices for culturally relevant science experiences.

STEM by Design by Anne Jolly (Routledge, 2016). This book shares tools to get started with STEM or enhance your current STEM program.

Teaching STEM in the Early Years by Sally Moomaw (Redleaf Press, 2013). This book includes activities that support STEM learning for young children.

Teaching STEM in the Preschool Classroom by Alissa A. Lange, Kimberly Brenneman, and Hagit Mano (Teachers College Press, 2019). This book helps educators bring STEM to life with young children.

Websites

Amoeba Sisters (youtube.com/@AmoebaSisters). Two sisters aim to demystify science with humor and relevance. They share videos, handouts, resources, and comics.

Bill Nye (billnye.com). Find all your favorite Bill Nye shows and books in one place.

Exploratorium (exploratorium.edu). The official website of the San Francisco Exploratorium museum shares resources for kids and educators.

NASA Kids' Club (nasa.gov/kidsclub). The NASA Kids' Club is a space for kids to play games, find at-home STEM activities, and learn about NASA. The website also shares resources for parents, teachers, and caregivers.

Nat Geo Kids (kids.nationalgeographic.com). This *National Geographic* website for kids shares games, videos, and more.

NOVA Labs (pbs.org/wgbh/nova/labs). NOVA Labs hosts STEAM activities and games for kids.

PBS Design Squad (pbskids.org/designsquad). This website includes STEAM games, activities, and videos for kids.

Project Noah (projectnoah.org). Project Noah is a global community for nature enthusiasts to share photographs and learn about wildlife.

Science Bob (sciencebob.com). Science Bob shares experiments, science fair ideas, science Q&As, videos, and more.

SciShow (youtube.com/c/SciShow). This YouTube channel explores the unexpected and helps people learn about the world around them and beyond.